The *Authority*
OF THE KINGDOM

God's River, the Kingdom

D R. ROBERT L. R O B I N S O N

Unless otherwise indicated, all scriptural quotations are from the King James Version of the Bible

The Authority of the Kingdom
Published by:
Robert Robinson Ministries
PO Box 10106
Cranston, RI 02910
ISBN 978-0-9747893-7-8

Copyright © 2007 by Robert L. Robinson

All rights reserved. No part of this book may be reproduced in any form, except for the inclusion of brief quotations in a review, without permission in writing from the author or publisher.

Printed in the United States of America

To the People of God everywhere, let us all embrace and begin to walk in the full Authority of the Kingdom
Dr. Robert L. Robinson

Table of Contents

Introduction i
The Kingdom 3
The Life of God Flowing 13
Fulfill the Time 19
Except they be agreed 29
The Prophet's Posture 39
The Authority in being sent 49
Your Kingdom Gift 55
Keepers 61
The Authority of the Kingdom 69

Introduction

The word *ignorance* denotes one's "lack of knowledge, learning and information." It is possible for a believer to be ignorant of the things of God, and that ignorance is displayed through the lacking of knowledge, learning, and information of God. Sadly to say, that is the standing of many believers, for they lack knowledge, learning, and, most importantly, information. The ignorance of an individual is power to the adversary, and the same is true to those within the kingdom of God. The less one refuses to know concerning God and His kingdom, the more of an advantage the enemy will have over that particular believer. A believer in the dark (walking in ignorance) will live a defeated life within the kingdom.

God has given His church, or His ekklesia, authority. What is authority? Authority is found in one Greek word as *exousia* (ex-oo-see'-ah), which speaks of the ability, right, or privilege to have control, so then *exousia* is authority given and the right and privileges to operate in that authority. There is another Greek word noted for the word authority, which is *katexousiazo* (kat-ex-oo-see-ad'-zo), which means "to have the full privilege or right to exercise authority." The Father has granted to the Body of Christ the privilege and right to exercise in His authority on earth, and this is the Authority of the Kingdom.

One's ignorance or refusing to seek God has brought about a time of despair and depravity. Many have been deprived because of their ignorance, which has allowed the enemy to deprive them. One's refusal to learn and seek God has sent the message that the status quo is the way the Father desires for His children to function, but nothing can be further from the truth. You as a believer must know who you are. Ignorance concerning the kingdom is unacceptable. This book serves as a message to all to remember who we are. It is also a warning to the believers all over the world to stop functioning beneath what the Father has called us into. As a believer you have a God-given right to function under the authority of the kingdom.

It is time to learn of the kingdom, and in the first chapter entitled "The Kingdom," there are five areas of the kingdom that will be discussed. Those areas are kingdom position, the kingdom character, the kingdom anointing and authority, kingdom glory, and kingdom harvest. Secondly, we will discuss the life of God flowing and what it will take to get that Life flowing through His people.

Much time has been wasted by many. The focus has been placed upon that which is not necessary. It has allowed the enemy to preoccupy God's people. In the third chapter we will learn of the importance of fulfilling the time. God requires an action on your part that would cause you to fill the time allotted to you for kingdom purpose.

A major dilemma within the body of Christ is marriages. Being married for many years has taught both Glenda and me many lessons. One of those lessons has been that in order to do kingdom work, it is important that we walk together. The Bible asks the question in Amos 3:3, "Can two walk together, except they be agreed?" If marriages are not together, it will cause a dilemma within the kingdom. A Christian marriage is prey for the enemy. Not functioning in the spirit of agreement will make it that must easier for the enemy to both attack and possibly destroy the relationship. We learn of our authority within the kingdom by knowing and functioning in what the Scriptures read.

One of the major gifts to function in this season is the prophet. God is getting ready to release prophets. However, prior to that releasing it will call for prophetic training amongst the Samuels of today. It will also require a particular posture as God is calling for the prophets of today to "put off thy shoes from off thy feet."

Divine order is God's divine accurate unchangeable arrangement in regards to His purpose, which cannot be altered. The divine order of God is noted in the authority of God seen in those who have been authorized and sent to a designated place. The father is calling for His church to function in the authority of the sent order. Your kingdom gift will operate to its fullest when it functions under the divine order of the Lord. The kingdom gift is that which was given to you from the Father. It is that gift that will cause an individual to be unique.

All that is written in this book serves as a prophecy to get the people of God to understand the Authority of the Kingdom. If the body of Christ as a whole can receive what the Holy Spirit is releasing, it will destroy the spirit of ignorance, defeat it and, most importantly, the believers will walk in full power. It's time to know Him, in the fellowship of His suffering. It's time to know about all of Him, for the more we know of Him the more powerful the believer becomes. The more powerful the believer becomes, the less powerful the enemy becomes. This will transpire when the people of God understand The Authority of the Kingdom and become His River.

The Kingdom
"The kingdom is graced"

The kingdom of God is here on earth. It is a living-breathing organism, started and anointed and appointed by the Father that it might expand. The word *kingdom* is the Greek word *basileia* (bas-il-i'-ah), which means "royalty and rule." The English word *kingdom* is made up of two words, *king* and *dom,* that mean "the dominion of the king." In essence the king has dominion here on earth. The kingdom is the rule and reign of God on earth through His People. His people are His kingdom, his extended hand and rule on earth. It is in the kingdom of God that is manifested in and through His people.

In this chapter entitled "The Kingdom," we will discuss five areas of the Kingdom. Because God has graced the kingdom, that gracing is supposed to create much success, success in every area the enemy has attempted to hold back. The five areas to be discussed will serve as an alarm to those who fail to realize just how much the Father has invested in the kingdom; also, it will cause many believers to understand the power and authority that we as a kingdom do possess.

> *Matthew 6:10*
> *Thy kingdom come. Thy will be done in earth, as it is in heaven.*

1. Kingdom Position

The first area to be discussed is the kingdom position. What is the position of the kingdom? Well, let's start by saying that it is not important for the world to understand the position of the kingdom; however, the church most definitely needs to understand the position of the kingdom. Jesus prayed in Matthew 6:10, "Thy kingdom come, thy will be done in earth as it is in heaven." The kingdom position is noted in this particular verse. The position of the kingdom is that the will of God is already determined and carried out by the inhabitants of the kingdom, just as the will of the King is done in heaven. The kingdom position of the will of God being done is the mode of operation. That mode is the position of the kingdom. We believe in allowing the will of God to be done to the fullest. The position is that God reigns here on earth through His people.

Luke 17:21
Neither shall they say, Lo here! or, lo there! for, behold, the kingdom of God is within you.

The kingdom of God is within the people of God. The meaning is, what is on the inside of the people of God manifests outside to the world. As previously stated, the world does not need to understand the kingdom, the church does. When the church understands that the kingdom is inside of us and needs to be manifested to the outside, the world will wonder of the kingdom because of the results of the kingdom work. Manifest the kingdom: pull out of you what God the Father has given you to do and manifest that.

The position of the kingdom is a sanctuary. What is a sanctuary? A sanctuary is a place for people who have lost hope. The position of the kingdom is that of a beacon light, a lighthouse, something that shows someone who is lost, the way to hope, freedom, liberty, and, most importantly, a sound mind. If the kingdom of God is within His people and the people are on earth, then the kingdom has taken up residence and position on earth. As the revelation of the kingdom expands within His people, the kingdom will expand as well.

Hosea 4:6
My people are destroyed for lack of knowledge: because thou hast rejected knowledge, I will also reject thee, that thou shalt be no priest to me: seeing thou hast forgotten the law of thy God, I will also forget thy children.

Wisdom is power, and the more one understands, the more power one will develop. Many believers are in a position that it does not allow them to be kingdom-minded. The reason being is because they lack the knowledge to understand what and who the kingdom is. In Hosea 4:6, there are two words that need to be addressed. The first word is *lack*, which is the Hebrew word *beliy* (bel-ee'), which means "failure." The second word needed to be discussed is the word *knowledge*, which is the Hebrew word *da`ath* (dah'-ath) which means, "to know." My people are destroyed for the *failure* to *know*. Failing to know anything can destroy anyone. Failing to know who you are in God will cause one to be a failure. Failure to understand and know the kingdom will cause one to live a defeated life. The desire to know the kingdom will produce wisdom, which will destroy the spirit of failure upon an individual. When you understand the position of the kingdom, you will walk in the power of that understanding.

John 8:31
Then said Jesus to those Jews which believed on him, If ye continue in my word, then are ye my disciples indeed;

The position of the kingdom is to produce believers who have a knowing of the power of God. Kingdom people must be disciples. They are to be discipled in the things of the kingdom. Knowing requires faith, to know something means to pursue it, then to have faith in what you have pursued and live in that revelation. Jesus said to the Jews who believed on him that if they continued in his word, then they are his disciples. The position of the kingdom is that when a person desires to know the kingdom, the kingdom will open up to that individual once he begins to seek the kingdom. When an individual continues in the word, then he is seeking the kingdom, seeking the information concerning the kingdom so that the enemy will not destroy him. So if one continues in His word as it pertains to the kingdom then he is my student or pupil truly. If one studies the kingdom and learn of the kingdom, he becomes a disciple of the kingdom. A disciple is one who is a replica of the original functioning under the authority of the kingdom.

The position of the kingdom is here on earth within the believer. Now the believer must seek the kingdom to know more of and understand the kingdom. When one understands the kingdom, then one can function in the power of the kingdom and not live a life of defeat but because of the kingdom live a life of victory. The position of the kingdom is that God rules and reigns on earth through His people.

2. **Kingdom character**

Rom. 14:17
For the kingdom of God is not meat and drink; but righteousness, and peace, and joy in the Holy Ghost.

The second area of the kingdom to be discussed is the character of the kingdom. What is the character of the kingdom? The kingdom of God consists of the righteousness of God, the peace of God, and the joy of God comprised in the Holy Ghost, which is in us. If the position of the kingdom is within the believer, then the believer also consists of the character of the kingdom. It is the righteousness of God. This is our standing in him. Then there is the peace of God. This is our mindset, our way of functioning and thinking. Then there is the joy of God which is our strength and motivation all of which are in the Holy Ghost, which is in the people of God.

The character of the kingdom is revealed through the citizens of the kingdom; therefore, the righteousness, peace, and joy should be seen in the kingdom by those who are outside the kingdom. It is a character that is noticed by the world, which in turn would cause others to wonder why they are able to feel and function the way that they do.

3. **Kingdom Anointing and Authority**

It is through the kingdom that the Hand of God is released that He might exercise His authority through His people on earth; God's being manifested through His people will reveal the "thy will be done on earth as it is in heaven."

The message of the kingdom takes precedence over anything. It comes and tears down anything that attempts to exalt itself above the knowledge of God. The message of the kingdom is a message to change the hearts and minds of those who are defeated. The kingdom is apostolic, meaning it is sent from heaven to a place called earth, and now the message of the kingdom must be preached or taught to those that they might be free. The Hand of God operates through His people in divine manifestation. Jesus said the kingdom of heaven is at hand, which means that the kingdom of heaven, the hand of God, is reaching out towards you: reach out and grab it.

If you don't understand the kingdom, then you will not know of the kingdom authority that the believer has here on planet earth. In 2 Corinthians 10:4 we reads, *"(For the weapons of our warfare are not carnal, but mighty through God to the pulling down of strong holds)"* The Greek word for warfare is *strateia* (strat-i'-ah). The word *strateia* comes from the root word *strateuomai*, which means "to *serve* in a military campaign; figuratively it means "to execute the apostolate." The weapon is a military strategy whose intent is to function with a warfare mentality, pull down strongholds, and destroy the works of the enemy. That is kingdom authority, which exists in the kingdom. The whole idea of 2 Corinthians 10:4-6 is one of apostolic anointing going into a region where there is no reverence or thought of God. The weapon of the apostolic is so mighty that it can pull down any type of ungodly mentality and bring that mentality into the obedience of Christ. The weapon of apostolic anointing is a kingdom anointing.

The kingdom anointing is a prison breaking, yoke destroying, stronghold breaking anointing that rests within and upon the kingdom of God. What is meant by strongholds? Strongholds speak of imprisonment, an imprisonment in the mind of an individual. A kingdom anointing then will destroy that hold on an individual. The kingdom anointing is an apostolic anointing. What is meant by apostolic anointing? The word *apostolic* is a derivative of the word *apostle*. The word *apostle* means "sent one," so *apostolic* means "one who operates under an anointing of being sent." Apostolic anointing is an anointing sent from heaven for now. Kingdom anointing rests upon apostolic people, meaning people who are sent to the kingdom for now, and their works will produce results within the kingdom.

4. **<u>Kingdom glory</u>**

   John 1:1-4
   In the beginning was the Word, and the Word was with God, and the Word was God. [2] The same was in the beginning with God. [3] All things were made by him; and without him was not any thing made that was made. [4] In him was life; and the life was the light of men.

The fourth area of the kingdom to be discussed is the kingdom glory. In John 1:4 it is important to understand that this passage was written to believers and that it gives a beautiful depiction of the kingdoms posture in regards to Christ. Verse four reads "*In him was life and the life was the light of men.*" In Jesus is the life, and that life is in men and within the kingdom. The revelation of Jesus is the light of the kingdom, and it is that life that is the breath of those within the kingdom. It is that same life that is extended to those who are in total darkness.

   John 1:14
   And the Word was made flesh, and dwelt among us, (and we beheld his glory, the glory as of the only begotten of the Father,) full of grace and truth.

In John 1:14, there is something to be noted concerning the church of God. The Bible reads "*and we beheld his glory*." What did the church do? The church beheld His glory. However, before the church could behold his glory, he first had to dwell among us. Now because he dwells among us, we behold his glory. This is the revelation of the Kingdom. The kingdom is God dwelling among us. The Word became flesh and dwelt among us. We beheld Him for who He really was. And so because we beheld him for who he really was or who he really is, he now lives amongst us. And amongst us is that life which is the light of men. That's the gospel of the kingdom.

Another word to be noted in verse fourteen is *beheld*. Whenever you see the word *beheld*, it denotes spirituality. The word *beheld* denotes something that is manifested to the natural eye but is actually taking place in the spirit realm. So when we behold him, we behold him *per se* in the spirit realm first, and what transpires in the spirit realm is then manifested or unveiled to the natural eye. The effects of the thing that took place in the spirit realm are manifested in the natural realm. The word *behold* denotes something happening in the spirit realm which will be manifested in the flesh.

> *Genesis 1:16*
> *And God made two great lights; the greater light to rule the day, and the lesser light to rule the night: he made the stars also.*

In Genesis 1:16 the greater light is to rule the day and the lesser light to rule the night. Greater light is Christ while the lesser light is the church. Why? Because the lesser light is the reflection of the greater light so that when He reigns, He reigns through the kingdom on earth. And even though there is darkness, the kingdom still reigns because the kingdom becomes that reflected light of Him (greater light) which brings that same light to a dark world.

> *Isaiah 6:3*
> *And one cried unto another, and said, Holy, holy, holy, is the Lord of hosts: the whole earth is full of his glory.*

The earth denotes the kingdom; the whole kingdom is full of His glory. The filling up of the kingdom is actually God filling up His people. He fills every area of the kingdom, and in doing so, when we are kingdom minded, then God fills every area of our lives, and all that is connected with us is affected by the filling up of God within His people. Because we allow him to fill himself, he runneth over. David said in the book of Psalms "*my cup runneth over.*" In other words, the very thing that houses the glory of the Lord in my life is running over. The Father fills His people with the glory of the kingdom, and in that filling He is running over in our lives. Because He is running over in our lives, He touches all that is connected with our lives, everything about the believer. Once the revelation of the kingdom is running over in your life, it will become kingdom oriented. The glory of the kingdom affects all that it touches; He affects us within the kingdom, then he flows out of us to that which is connected to us and affects that. The flow and filling of God will affect everything about you. He overflows you flowing down to the outside of you, flowing down to everything that you touch and all that is connected to you that is touched by the Father running over in your life now becomes kingdom oriented. Your walk with God, your prayer time, your home, sacrifice, money, children, and even your employment all become kingdom oriented.

The word then becoming flesh means the word being manifested in the midst of his people. If the word is not manifested, then we will never behold the glory of the Lord. Kingdom people can get as much God as they desire, but they will have to be free enough to allow God to be free through them. If you are limited in allowing God to be free, guess what? He is limited. You can get as much of God as you want or as little of God as you want. But to behold him means that he has dwelt among his people fully no hindrances for He has *pleroo* (play-ro'-o), which is one of the Greek words for "filled," and it means basically to fill every crack and crevice; He has filled with the glory of the kingdom, every area of the kingdom affecting the kingdom people, which in turn affects all that we possess.

5. <u>Kingdom Harvest</u>

Matthew 13:44
Again, the kingdom of heaven is like unto treasure hid in a field; the which when a man hath found, he hideth, and for joy thereof goeth and selleth all that he hath, and buyeth that field.

The kingdom of heaven is like unto a treasure hid in a field. The man was searching the field and found a pearl. What did the man do? He hid the pearl and went and sold all that he had so that he would purchase the field. The field denotes the kingdom, and the man selling everything that he had denotes he letting everything else go. Jesus said to seek ye first the kingdom. The man selling all that he had in order to purchase the kingdom is a man that had to let everything else go because all that he had prior to the kingdom, when he found the kingdom those things had no more value. He found value in the pearl. The pearl denotes potential. The man had to let some things go. God desires for His people to operate in kingdom, which will in turn fulfill the next part of Matthew 6:33, which is the *"and all these things shall be added unto you."* If we seek the kingdom first, and release God within the earth realm, then God will add some things to our lives that we have been trying to work for and have been unsuccessful. The man found a pearl in the kingdom!

> *Joel 2:23*
> *Be glad then, ye children of Zion, and rejoice in the Lord your God: for he hath given you the former rain moderately, and he will cause to come down for you the rain, the former rain, and the latter rain in the first month.*

The prophet Joel speaks of two types of rain, for it's going to take two types of rain in order to get a kingdom harvest. The former rain represents a season of rain that prepares the ground. It will rain so much that it will cause the ground to be ready for planting. The former rain denotes a type of word for a particular time in the season. A former rain word is a preparation word, a word that prepares for harvest.

Then there is the latter rain. The latter rain is a rain for the actual harvest. This is another type of word for a season, a word that will nurture that which was previously planted and produce a kingdom harvest. Both the former and latter rain denotes a season and time for planting and harvesting. This type of rain, prophetically speaking, is a latter and former rain, which is called kingdom rain. The kingdom rain is going to break up all that is not kingdom-oriented in your life (latter rain, rain for preparation) and then release another rain, which is a word that will make the ground ready for breakthrough and harvest. A former rain is a former word that makes the ground ready; a latter rain will bring forth a kingdom harvest.

The kingdom of God is the Spirit of Him living within His people. Its territory is the earth and the heart of the believer. The people have the kingdom within them which needs to be manifested in earth (Luke 17:21). The Kingdome of God consists of His vision, purpose, destiny, dunamis, Word, and faith. Concerning His vision, the people of God need to produce His will on earth. Concerning the purpose, the people of the Kingdom need to understand their reason for existence; concerning His destiny, the people of the Kingdom need to understand the importance of their operating to their fullest. Concerning

His Dunamis, the people of the kingdom need to realize the power and authority given them. The dunamis power is the miracle working power of God working through them. Concerning the Word, the people of the kingdom must realize that the Word is faith in action, the word is the Gospel of Christ, and it is God in full demonstration. Concerning faith, the people of the kingdom must have the God-kind of faith working within the kingdom, which will allow the kingdom to advance unhindered.

As previously discussed, the five areas of the kingdom are Kingdom Position, Kingdom character, Kingdom anointing and Authority, Kingdom glory, and Kingdom Harvest. It is within these five areas that the Father has graced the kingdom and His people. It is through these areas that if functioned fully will bring kingdom results in a mega way.

The Life of God Flowing
"God's River, the Kingdom"

Rev. 2:29
He that hath an ear, let him hear what the Spirit saith unto
the churches.

The Scripture reads, "for the word of God is quick and powerful." The Word of God just needs something to rest which is the believers' spirit. Once that word rests in the spirit of the believer, that word causes that believer to come that much more alive. The Word of God is prophetical, meaning it constantly speaks and reveals a prophetic word into the life of an individual. *"He that hath an ear, let him hear."* What does the scripture tell the believer to do? The believer is instructed to hear because hearing is necessary in order to become; when the word of God is heard, it is the responsibility of the believer to operate in application and apply what is heard. The Bible speaks and continues to speak to the people of God, imploring them to hear what the spirit is saying.

When I was a newly saved believer, many of those from the church taught that because I was newly born again, it would be better for me to stay away from the Old Testament. I'm sure they meant well; the early church leaders were afraid that I along with many other newly born again believers would be confused and therefore discouraged by reading the Old testament and not understanding it. They meant well, and to this day I love many of my forefathers of the Gospel who have gone home to be with the Lord. But the Word of God is powerful, and because it is so powerful, it will not allow me to become discouraged or confused because confusion is not the spirit of God. There is much truth, much revelation in the Old Testament, and I definitely found a powerful word from the Lord in the book of Isaiah.

Genesis 1:11
And God said, Let the earth bring forth grass, the herb
yielding seed, and the fruit tree yielding fruit after his kind,
whose seed is in itself, upon the earth: and it was so.

In Genesis 1:11 there is to be noted a progression, a forward movement. From the earth, God calls for the green; then out of the green came the seed and fruit bearing trees. Note the progression: out of something comes something, and out of that something comes something. One thing causes another to exist. Out of water comes dry land; there's always something that comes out of something that comes out of something that comes out of something; out of God comes Jesus His Son, and out of Jesus comes the Church.

In the book of Genesis, out of the first day comes the second day, and from the second day comes the third. Note that there can be no third without the second and there can be no second without the first; everything comes out of something else in order to exist.

Let us look at Genesis 1:11 prophetically. The earth brought forth grass, herb-yielding seed after his kind, and the tree yielding fruit was within itself after his kind and God saw that it was good. The seed denotes you, the believer, while the earth or dirt represents pastoral leadership, your covering. The seed must be planted into the earth; the believer needs covering and needs to be covered by something that possesses what the seed needs. Scientifically speaking, dirt possesses a nutrient needed for seed; prophetically speaking, the dirt that covers the believer possesses a nutrient that the believer need, so, God plants you in the ministry where you can be covered because that ministry or pastoral covering is what you need. There is something in your covering that you need to help you to mature and to become the thing that God has ordained you to become. That's why the pastor watches out for your soul. Why? Because there are certain things that God has provided that pastor with that will help you and mature you. I personally would never sit under anyone who could not cover me enough to coach me into my purpose.

> *Isaiah 43:19*
> *Behold, I will do a new thing; now it shall spring forth; shall ye not know it? I will even make a way in the wilderness, and rivers in the desert.*

There is always planting; God planted his Son; the church is planted in order that it might produce. When we speak of planting, it denotes a placing. God places the believers where they need to be planted or placed. Note Isaiah 43:19, where the Lord said, "Behold I will do a new thing." The word *new* is the Hebrew word *chadash* (khaw-dawsh'), that means "fresh." Behold I will do a "fresh" thing. What is the fresh thing the Father will do? The fresh thing is you, the believer, the fresh creation of God.

The scripture goes on to say, "Now it shall spring forth." The word *spring* is the Hebrew word *tsamach* (tsaw-makh'), which means "to sprout or to come forth as a bud." Let's put this together: a believer must understand that being pastored is important. Prophetically speaking, the pastor is the dirt, which covers and nourishes the believer. The believer is the fresh thing that must go through process but will eventually sprout or spring forth. When you are ready for kingdom ministry, the Father will cause you to spring up; He will launch you.

"*I will even make a way in the wilderness, and rivers in the desert.*" It is in this verse that we get the task of the kingdom. The Word states the Father will make a way in the wilderness and rivers in the desert. The desert is a very dry, desolate place that has absolutely no life; the desert represents the world. The Father says He will place rivers in that desert. The rivers are the kingdom, and in the kingdom, the Father is going to have the called to function in inhumane conditions and not be moved by what we see. The river of God will flow to the dry areas of the lives of lost people and bring life.

> *Genesis 2:10*
> *And a river went out of Eden to water the garden; and from thence it was parted, and became into four heads.*

Who is the River? The River is the Kingdom. The Kingdom is going to be placed in dark, dry places and cause moisture to come. There was a river that came out of Eden and parted into four heads. The number four denotes the world, and the river of God will flow into the four corners of the earth and touch the world. This is the kingdom. The river came out of the church and parted into four heads. Water flowed to different areas of the earth and that flow of the river brought life to the desert.

> *Ezekiel 47:1*
> *Afterward he brought me again unto the door of the house; and, behold, waters issued out from under the threshold of the house eastward: for the forefront of the house stood toward the east, and the waters came down from under from the right side of the house, at the south side of the altar.*

The Father is calling for prayer; it is prayer time within the Kingdom. Here in Ezekiel 47 we need to see what the Holy Spirit is teaching in this verse; prophetically speaking, we need to see what

Ezekiel saw. The prophet was taken to the door of the house and waters issued out from under the threshold of the house eastward. The waters denote the kingdom, the believers those who have been processed, those who understood the importance of remaining in the dirt until the Father sprang them forth. These waters were created through the spirit of prayer, and it is the prayer that pushed the water out from the four walls of the church.

> *Ezekiel 47:5*
> *Afterward he measured a thousand; and it was a river that I could not pass over: for the waters were risen, waters to swim in, a river that could not be passed over.*

The waters became a river. The river was so large that the prophet could not pass by; the waters were risen and to deep too swim through. This denotes the Kingdom aligning itself with the will of the Father. This river noted in verse five is a coming forth of the Kingdom, large enough to be recognized and noticed by all.

> *Ezekiel 47:8-9*
> *Then said he unto me, These waters issue out toward the east country, and go down into the desert, and go into the sea: which being brought forth into the sea, the waters shall be healed. And it shall come to pass, that every thing that liveth, which moveth, whithersoever the rivers shall come, shall live: and there shall be a very great multitude of fish, because these waters shall come thither: for they shall be healed; and every thing shall live whither the river cometh.*

Remember in Isaiah 43:19 the Lord said that He would place a river in the desert. In the desert is dryness, death, and it is to that place that the Father is calling for life to come. Life is going to come by means of the River. The waters flowed towards the desert and were to flow to the sea. The sea was sick and needed to be cured, so the River Kingdom of God flowed towards the sea and the sea was healed. The fish in the sea were sick, and the River was able to heal the fish. The Kingdom River was able to meet the needs of all that it touched. The River of God came forth and operated in its purpose. The kingdom or River of God is God in full demonstration.

At this time within the Kingdom, the body of Christ needs to prepare to see God manifested in what we say. I will repeat that: the body of Christ needs to prepare to see God manifested in what we say.

No more praying prayers for God to move at a certain time and in the back of our minds we're actually praying a prayer of doubt asking God to move when He feels up to it. No, when the River flows and operates in true anointing God will back up His River; the River will operate in the impossible.

The River will be placed in positions of impossibilities, and God will prove Himself. In the River it will be a God-given opportunity that he has given you that he might show himself through you. Today the Church must become kingdom, and the mindset of the kingdom is "I can do all things through Christ who is my strength." The River will accomplish all that God has set for it to do through Christ, who is the strength of the River. In the River is life; in the River is resurrection power.

I see a River, a river that will not flow according to who and where it wants but a river whose wind gives the direction of its flow. That wind is an Eastward wind of the Holy Spirit. I see a River flowing into the desert-dry desolate, run-down lives of individuals who have given up hope. I see a river flowing into various lifestyles and cleansing those lifestyles. I see a River flowing on the most unholy day of the year, operating in revival. I see a River so large and so powerful that the enemy has to think twice about attempting to cross it. I see a River that consists of the love, power, and faithfulness of God. I see a River flowing to same-sex marriages, drowning that spirit; I see a river so strong that the hold which the enemy had on that situation will be broken. I see a River flowing into hospitals healing incurable diseases; I see a river that will cause the local church to become mega, not mega in natural abilities and accomplishments, but mega in the power of God.

Mark 1:15
And saying, The time is fulfilled, and the kingdom of God is at hand: repent ye, and believe the gospel.

The kingdom of God is at hand, meaning the kingdom is within your reach. All you have to do is, when the River flows, reach out and grab it. The River will consist of all that is needed for God to be glorified in and through ministry. The River of God will touch our children, and the River will affect them, they will operate in an anointing that will stop the enemy in his tracks. It is the children who will not be ashamed of the Gospel but will believe in the Gospel. They will not be robots, we will not have to threaten them, but they will have a love for God.

The believer must realize how necessary it will be to become obedient and listen to the prophetic voice of that which covers them. The pulpit is going to be the most important place, for the pulpit is the threshold where the water will begin to take form and begin to flow outward.

The River of God is strategically coming together hearing what God is saying. The Father is saying that the seas and fishes are contaminated, and everything in it is dying or dead. Not only does it denote the world but it denotes different areas of the church. So the Father is equipping a people who understand the importance of being developed, who understand the importance of functioning in the kingdom. And it is those people that are going to part into four heads; it will be those who will flow out of the four walls of comfort and flow into the desert place.

Commitment is the key; what are you willing to be committed to? One cannot just go to church and not have a desire to be committed. If one is not committed to what God is speaking, it means one is not in agreement. Corporately speaking, the body must be committed to what the Father is calling forth, and that calling forth is a River. You will only be successful in what God has called you to do.

Fulfill the Time
"Kairos and Chronos"

There are three stages of a prophetic word; the first stage is to hear it. The second stage of a prophetic word is preparation; after you hear what God is saying, then you must prepare for what God said. The third stage of the prophetic is manifestation; once you have prepared for it, then you become that Word. This is full manifestation. Many believers often get caught between the stages of hearing and preparing, and what happens is that most develop a conversation of what God has said, but there was never an action from the individual in regards to what God said. The conversation becomes, "Well, the Lord promised me over thirty years ago, and I'm still waiting." No, you became caught in a time span; you're caught between the two stages of hearing and preparation, never coming into the third stage, which is the full manifestation of what God promised.

> Gal. 4:4
> *But when the fulness of the time was come, God sent forth his Son, made of a woman, made under the law,*

In Galatians 4:4 let us notice the words "fullness of time." What is the fullness of time? The word *fullness* is the Greek word *pleuroma*, which denotes a filling as in to fill a container. The root word is *full*; however, the actual word *pleuroma* denotes an act of filling something. The fullness of time is the filling of time. The word for *time* is the Greek word *chronos*, which is "time allotted in order to fulfill your purpose." Notice in the Scripture in Galatians that when the fullness of time was come, God did an act, He sent forth His Son. This reveals to us that the filling of time (or time allotted to you by God) requires an action on one's part. Time became filled with an action on the Father's part by sending forth His Son.

The filling of time needs to operate in your purpose according to the time allotted you. The three stages of a prophetic word are necessary because they operate in chronos, or time, allotted you. The fullness of time is actually the believers fulfilling what God has called them into. What is that time to be filled with? That time is to be filled with you operating in your purpose. What is your purpose? Your purpose is the kingdom-oriented charge from God to you, which will cause you to affect not only the kingdom but the world. Your purpose is different from those in the world; you were given a charge to manifest God in earth.

Many are still living their lives in the first dimension of a prophetic word never reacting to what God said. A completely obeyed (3 stages) prophetic word always connects with times and seasons because it is through time that God manifests His agenda.

Chronos is time allotted to you, and it is needed in order to function and complete *kairos*. What is *kairos*? *Kairos* is another word for time, however, this word denotes a time or season of opportunity. Time allotted (*chronos*) works along with time of opportunity (*kairos*). Right now in the kingdom, the Father has released a *kairos* and a *chronos*; He has given the church the time and the opportunity to function within the kingdom. Therefore the church must be aware of the time.

If an individual has to be at h is place of employment by 8:00 a.m., there must be time allowed in order to travel and arrive at the place of employment on time. *Kairos* is the opportunity to work; chronos is the time allotted you to arrive at work in order to take advantage of the kairos (opportunity) and make a living. Because the opportunity has been given to you, it is important that you govern yourself accordingly and not be late. If you are late continuously, it means you have no regard for time (kairos), the opportunity given you.

You don't want to be late producing in the kingdom; you want to take advantage of the *kairos*, so that you govern yourself and honor the *chronos* given you because the kingdom always operates on time, for time in the kingdom is always "now."

Many do not understand the important concept of God's timing in the kingdom. The bible speaks of timing; it speaks of days, months, years, seasons and so on. If you miss your season, then you could end up waiting an awful long time for another one. You have only operated in one stage of the prophetic, we only heard and never prepared; in essence, the believer does not act upon what God has said.

Many have planted gardens, but that garden did not just appear; it required some work. The desire to have a garden came first; this speaks of a type of hearing. Then the ground had to be turned over or tilled; the ground needed to be broken up. After it was broken up, then seed needed to be planted, then the garden watered; this speaks of preparation (the second stage). Thirdly, after a few weeks there was a manifestation, that which was planted matured and pushed through the earth; this speaks of full manifestation, becoming what was purposed. This is how the prophetic works; it will take work and hard work, but eventually the purposed thing will appear and that purposed thing will bring glory to the kingdom of God.

How many of you are sick and tired of not being happy doing what God called you to do? My desire is to see God's people come to full maturity, to be blessed; I want to see preachers become trained walking in the power and the authority of God. I want to see people set free. None of this will happen if believers continue to just sit back and talk about it but do nothing. The mentality of "Well, we are waiting on the Lord" IS NOT GOING TO WORK! God will give you whatever you need in order to be successful within the kingdom; however, God is not going to do all of the work; there must be a preparation in order to manifest. God will give you or supply what you need in order to carry out his purpose, but there's one thing that He will not do. He will not do the work for you, for you must prepare and manifest.

God has given to every man a measure of faith; however, He will not give him application. Application comes from you, the believer; you must apply what God gives you. God will not make you apply your faith, and you must have the will for application. God will give you everything that you need in order to be successful, except the applying of your ability; He has given you ability, but he will not make you apply that ability. You must have the faith to apply that ability that God has given you.

1 Sam. 17:23
And as he talked with them, behold, there came up the champion, the Philistine of Gath, Goliath by name, out of the armies of the Philistines, and spake according to the same words: and David heard [them].

In 1 Samuel 17:23, Goliath was standing between both camps; he was the champion of the Philistines, and he was down in the midst of the valley. The Philistines are on one side of the mountain while Israel was on the other, and Goliath is in the middle. Goliath held up Israel for forty days, and, finally, David arrived asking what was going on. Here is my question: Who was anointed to slay the giant? My answer is, "Anyone who was bold enough to apply his or her faith as David did." It was anybody who had faith enough in God, enough to step up to the plate. The difference between David and his brother at this time is that David applied what he believed. David had enough God and enough faith in him to believe God and step up to the plate; he was anointed to be king and now it was time to prepare, and part of that preparation was David demonstrating just who God was through him.

> *James 2:26*
> *For as the body without the spirit is dead, so faith without works is dead also.*

Faith without works is dead. What is the difference between faith and works? Faith is your belief while works is the applying of that belief. Faith without works is dead, which means that regardless of how much faith one has, if one doesn't apply faith then the request is dead. So works is the application of your faith. You cannot only believe in God; you've got to apply that belief. God gives the believer what he needs. He gives ability, the money, the land, and whatever else that is needed to get the work for the kingdom done; however, the Father will not give application of those things. The application is the works which must be done by the individual whom God has equipped.

As believers we must be careful not to become stuck in a dimension looking for another day because a continuous look for another day without faith and works will never come because we sat and did nothing but comforted one another in what he has said. Maybe most of our hang up has been not applying our abilities. If God has given you the ability to do something and you do not do it, that means you lack faith in the ability that God has given you.

I always remind my church, House of Manna Ministries, that God is not going to turn our ministry into a robot, meaning the ministry must operate because it has a desire to do the will of God. The ministry must be broken enough to pray the will of God and to become that will and with an open heart, with pure hands, with a pure mind, carry out what the Father has anointed us to do. The worst thing that we can become is a people that stay in one state or dimension of hearing God only and not preparing.

The worst thing that a believer can become is a church member and not a child of the kingdom. Because if you are a child of the kingdom, you will think like the king, you will see like the king, and your desires will be like the kings desire, and that's a principle. If an individual sits back and dreams of success but never does anything about it, then that dream will become a sad, overly rehearsed song.

While Joseph was in the prison, he was still given a *kairos* (opportunity); he was able to interpret dreams. While he is in prison for a crime that he did not commit, he still functions in *kairos* (opportunity) and *chronos* (time allotted him). Even through dark times, bad times, terrible times, he still operated in his gift. Why did he continue to operate in his gift? Because he understood that God told him something; he dreamed something, and regardless of what his brothers said, he knew his brothers were unhappy but continued to operate until what God said would come to pass. Joseph held on until he came into his manifestation; he fulfilled his time.

Remember, God will give you the ability, but He will not do the work for you. At the time of this writing, I would have published over twenty books. Now, I could have written the manuscripts and left them on my computer and nothing would have ever come of those writings. I acted upon what God gave me. He gave me the ability, he gave me *kairos* (opportunity), and he gave me *chronos* (time to work in *kairos*). I could have sat there and said "Oh wait I'm waiting for a day when I get a book deal." If a book deal comes it comes, if it does not then it doesn't but one thing I am going to do, I am stepping out on faith. God gives the land, he'll give the seed, He will give you the ability, but He will not give you application. What I am doing is fulfilling the time.

> *Ephes. 1:4*
> *According as he hath chosen us in him before the foundation of the world, that we should be holy and without blame before him in love:*

The kingdom of God is the rule and reign of God through you, the believer, on planet earth. The kingdom is where the believers live; they live in the kingdom. When did he choose you? All that you could ever be in him was already predetermined before the foundation of the earth. God chose you and because He has chosen you, there is more to your relationship with God than for you to come to church and bring your Bible under your arm. No. There's more to this walk and relationship than that. It's about your whole make up, your whole idea, your whole gift. Understand that you were chosen, which means you were preordained; your whole walk, call, and anointing were already in the mind of God. God knew and chose you! Your calling and gifting are unique, and what you have to offer to the kingdom is unique. God thought you out before you went through the dirt, the hell, the high water. God already predetermined who you would be in Him. So your gifting was not something that you chose. It was something that God gave you. It is that gift, your God-given gift, that fits within the kingdom, and it is that gift that will make room for what you have to carry out. As you carry out what God has called and gifted you to do, you will be fulfilling the time!

The enemy thought he had you depressed because it appears as though you did not fit within the kingdom, and this was partly the reason for your hearing God but not preparing for God, but the devil is a liar, and God is calling for you now. God has already thought of you these last eons of years. Your ugly life proclaimed to you from the enemy is not your make up but is only the picture that the enemy has attempted to paint over your life.

> *1 Cor. 10:13*
> *There hath no temptation taken you but such as is common to man: but God is faithful, who will not suffer you to be tempted above that ye are able; but will with the temptation also make a way to escape, that ye may be able to bear it.*

> *Romans 12:7*
> *Or ministry, let us wait on our ministering: or he that teacheth, on teaching;*

The enemy will call you everything that the Father has not. Sitting in one dimension doing nothing is a perfect opportunity for the enemy to speak to you in your sealed house, but I hear the Lord saying, "It's the fullness of time, and now come out from among them." Who are "them?" They are the non-believers who cannot see who you are in the spirit! Your strength is determined by you finding out who you really are in the word. The scripture reads that *"but God is faithful, who will not suffer you to be tempted above that ye are able."* Can that scripture mean that when the enemy told you that you were at your breaking point, you actually were not? Can that scripture mean that when you thought you couldn't take it anymore you actually could because it was God who was sustaining you? Could it mean that though you are in the midst of turmoil, God has already made you a way of escape? It means exactly that because God is faithful. The way of escape is your focusing on who and what the Father has called you into and for you to function in that capacity.

Romans 12:6-8
Having then gifts differing according to the grace that is given to us, whether prophecy, let us prophesy according to the proportion of faith; [7] Or ministry, let us wait on our ministering: or he that teacheth, on teaching; [8] Or he that exhorteth, on exhortation: he that giveth, let him do it with simplicity; he that ruleth, with diligence; he that sheweth mercy, with cheerfulness.

In Romans 12:6-8 we note that God has graced the believers with differing gifts. The word *differing* is the Greek word *diaphoros* (dee-af'-or-os), which means "various or different." Because the Father has given differing gifts to the believers, one cannot measure success by another because we are graced and anointed to do different things within the kingdom. That's right. You the believer are anointed to function within the kingdom. The problem is that there are those who do not apply those gifts, and because of non-application, it causes many to walk in unbelief and doubt. A good example of this is when faith is operating in the believer, and unbelief sets in and severs the relationship that a person had with faith and, therefore, causes one to no longer walk in faith but doubt. The reason is that the faith relationship has been separated.

Romans 12:7 states, "*or ministry let us wait on our ministering.*" This passage has been misunderstood through the years, and because of this many have been misled. Many taught that the word *wait* means to stop and literally wait for your time to minister. The words "*let us wait*" are italicized, which denotes it is not in the original. It should read, "*On ministry give yourself to ministry.*" The word *wait* does not mean to sit down and become complacent until the Lord does something. It is time for you to begin to function in what you have been called and graced to do and wait in that or serve in that capacity. Give yourself over to ministry, or give yourself over to the calling so that you can fulfill the time.

Man has gotten caught up in what God has told them but never prepared for what He told them, which has caused them to be stuck between stages of a prophetic word. Many are sitting back doing nothing, and in between that we become bored, and what we do becomes stale. It becomes stale to you because you become out of sync. You went through a season of hearing, but you stayed too long. You were supposed to go through a season of hearing then a season of preparation. God has given you everything that is needed for you to function in the kingdom; however, as previously stated, God will not give you application.

The results of what you do are recognized by the world. The Bible reads, *"Let your light so shine before men, that they may see your good works, and glorify your Father which is in heaven"* (Matt. 5:16). Men will see the good works, and regardless of how they believe, they cannot deny the good work that is in you and thereby glorify the Father. In other words, the testimony of God is how you handle what God has given you to do. The testimony of the Lord is your being obedient and working out or bringing out what He has given you. Let your light so shine before men; let your calling, your gifting, your anointing be seen in the presence of the world. Do it in the midst of the scoffers, the haters, and the liars who say all manner of evil against you; let your light so shine; operate within the kingdom of God in the midst of the non-believers so that they see the good work about you. Let them come to you and say, "It has got to be of God."

The gifting that you have is orchestrated or given by God. God has orchestrated the calling and purpose that you walk in or are supposed to be walking in right now; He took the time to design it specifically for you.

In regards to my personal life, why have I written so many books? Because that's what the Father has given me to do to leave a record, a word for the people of God so that they can understand the walking not only in righteousness, peace, and joy in the Holy Ghost, but walking in the full authority of the kingdom.

Many feel as though they understand the purpose and meaning of the kingdom, but they don't. Because if they understood then we would see the results of their works. If we understood the kingdom fully, we would operate in that realm of manifestation. When we understand the kingdom fully, God Himself will have the ability to get inside His Church and flow out. When we understand the kingdom, God will function in the midst of his people, and the people will be free enough to allow God to be God. It is then that the Church becomes the tabernacle of God. His name is Emanuel. What does *Emanuel* mean? It means "amongst us, with us and through us is our God who reigns." That's Emmanuel. Where He lives in the midst of his people and regardless of what we are faced with, our worship, our praise is not according to how we feel, but it's according to who God is. That's the kingdom.

The fulfilling of time calls for an action; God sent forth His son. Now, an action is required of you, the believer. God spoke a word, and you did hear that word. Now is time to get up and prepare. As you prepare, you will see God begin to take form in you and with your gifting in a particular area; God will be glorified and men will have to glorify the Father because of what He has anointed and sanctioned for you to do within the kingdom. Fulfill the time!

Except They Be Agreed
"Kingdom Marriages"

Statistics state that Christian divorce and worldly divorce statistically are the same. Why is there such a problem with Christian marriages? One of the major problems with Christian marriages is not understanding each other. It has been my experience that preachers who are married to other preachers fall into this category because both feel they have a call to fulfill, and rightfully so. The negative side to that is that both become so occupied with attempting to fulfill their call, that their relationship goes lacking. Each individual in the marriage fails to recognize each other's call within the kingdom, which in many situations leads to divorce. Many marriages have failed because of the lack of communication, understanding, and understanding each other's anointing and call to the body of Christ.

In the case where both are preachers, it appears as though each has an agenda to do the will of the Lord; however, they forget to include each other. Their hearts desire is to please God, walk upright, be obedient, serve the Lord, and to operate in purpose. The desire to please God is easy to come by; however, the act of pleasing God is a horse of a different color because the action of pleasing God requires changes, and if a mate doesn't understand where he or she is going in God, the necessary changes needed to be made in ministry, which in turn will have to be made in the marriage, will create controversy. Change always upsets ideas, plans, and, most importantly, desire.

In this chapter we will look at understanding how important it is for marital relationships to function in accordance with the call of the kingdom and how necessary it is for each couple to function in that call without neglecting that marital relationship within the kingdom. In other words, we need to understand how important it is to be able to do kingdom work and remain happy and fulfilled in the home.

In the book of first Samuel, everyone has a tendency to talk of Hannah, including me. We look at what Hannah went through with Penninah, we look at how Hannah desired a son whom she vowed to give back to the Lord, but we fail to notice the relationship and commitment of Elkanah, her husband, to Hannah. Elkanah was a Godly man who loved his wife, Hannah. Elkanah felt her pain of not having a child; he felt the pain of Hannah being barren, yet he loved her. In 1 Samuel 1:8, Elkanah noticed that Hannah was upset and he attempts to comfort her by saying *"am I not worth ten sons?"* Relationships within the kingdom between marital couples will require that both individuals be concerned and ministerial in each other's personal battles and shortcomings. Elkanah, a godly man, was not too godly to not care for the condition and pain of his wife.

> 1 Samuel 1:19
> *And they rose up in the morning early, and worshipped before the Lord, and returned, and came to their house to Ramah: and Elkanah knew Hannah his wife; and the Lord remembered her.*

When it was time for worship, Hannah along with Elkanah rose up in the morning early and worshipped before the Lord and then returned to Ramah. When they returned home to Ramah, then Elkanah knew Hannah his wife. Note the connection, Elkanah was with Hannah in all that she went through; when Hannah went to Shiloh to worship, Elkanah traveled with her. My point is, Elkanah knew Hannah's desire and he walked with Hannah wherever she went meaning they were together in the situation, Hannah did not have to go at this alone because it was both Hannah and Elkanah's situation.

Hannah eventually conceived and had a son and called him Samuel. Elkanah and his house went up to offer unto the Lord the yearly sacrifice; Hannah remained home because she wanted to wean the child first before bringing him to Shiloh. Elkanah said, *"Do what seemeth thee good; tarry until thou have weaned him."* Again, look at the attitude of Elkanah. He understood the heart of Hannah, and he does not stand in her way, the reason being is that he understands what Hannah went through and what she promised God. In all actuality, both Elkanah and Hannah had to be in agreement concerning the promise to give the boy back to God.

Hannah finally arrives in Shiloh, and she leaves the child there that he may minister before the Lord. In 1 Samuel 2:11, Elkanah went to Ramah and the child did minister unto the Lord; however it is important to note that Hannah could not have made the decision to give Samuel back to the Lord without the consent of her husband, Elkanah. Elkanah's and Hannah's decision was kingdom oriented. The child was to function in the kingdom; therefore, both parents had to understand what was necessary for the kingdom, not what they wanted for their personal lives. God had a purpose and plan for that which came out of Hannah. Even Hannah being barren was prophetic because the Bible says that the Lord had shut up her womb and because the Lord shut up

Hannah's womb, only the Lord could open it. It was prophetic; Hannah could not get pregnant until the Lord was ready for her to get pregnant. It was the fulfilling, or the filling up, of time in the life of Hannah and Elkanah. It was necessary that the family situation to be in order. It was important that Elkanah understand who Hannah was; he also had to understand what Hannah went through. Elkanah had to also understand that what came out of Hanna belonged to the Lord. All that was being done was weighing on the obedience and understanding of Elkanah because he was Hannah's husband. Both loved God, both believed God, both understood the importance of worship, both understood the importance of sacrifice, and both understood the importance of giving the very thing that they desired back to God! Because they were in agreement with each other and the Lord, the Lord blessed them with three more children. Believers within the kingdom must know what takes precedence in their lives and marriage as it pertains to the kingdom.

> *1 Peter 3:7*
> *Likewise, ye husbands, dwell with them according to knowledge, giving honour unto the wife, as unto the weaker vessel, and as being heirs together of the grace of life; that your prayers be not hindered.*

As we continued to receive this revelation concerning marriages within the kingdom, let us look at 1 Peter 3:7. The word for knowledge is the Greek word *gnosis* (gno'-sis), which means "an intelligent recognition of the nature of the marriage relationship." Peter teaches that it is important to dwell with a mate, but it is just as important to have knowledge or an intelligent recognition of who the mate is. Once it is understood as to what is recognized in the mate, then one is to give honour to that individual. Once the gift and call is recognized within both individuals, each needs to honor the other for who they are within the kingdom.

The Scripture goes on to state that the wife is the weaker vessel. The word *weaker* denotes the physical condition of the wife. Let's look at the word for *vessel*. The word for *vessel* is the Greek word *skeuos* (skyoo'-os), which means "a vessel, implement, equipment or apparatus." In all actuality *vessel* here speaks of different articles of the furniture within the house of God. Prophetically speaking, they both are pieces of furniture or equipment utilized within the kingdom. Both vessels within the marriage are called, chosen articles for the sake of the kingdom. Each vessel needs to recognize each other's placement in the kingdom; both have a place, and none is greater than the other. Once this is recognized within both individuals within the marriage, then the prayers of the individuals will not be hindered, cut into or interrupted.

Formed vs. Made

Genesis 2:6
But there went up a mist from the earth, and watered the whole face of the ground.

As we look at Genesis 2:6, there is something to note prophetically. A mist went up from the earth. The mist was in Eden, which denotes the kingdom. The word *Eden* means delight, which gives a beautiful view of the church. Eden represents the church of God. The mist is described in the Hebrew as the word *'ed* (ade), which means "an enveloping fog." With this particular word, it is important to note the action of the word in order to get the understanding of the word. The action of a fog covers, acts, and looks like a type of smoke. There was a mist or smoke in the garden. The mist or smoke denotes praise and worship. In the middle of the Garden (kingdom) was a mist or a smoke which was constant praise and worship. Praise is the heartbeat and center of the kingdom; the praises of God in His Eden keep Eden watered and moist.

The message of the kingdom and also the effects of that message will be seen and heard throughout the universe. The enemy will use every dirty tactic that he can in order to stop the voice of the Kingdom. When I started this chapter I began to talk about the importance of marriages and within those marriages that each mate understands who they are within the kingdom as it pertains to ministry. Kingdom marital couples must also understand each other's position. In this part of the chapter we are going to deal with the kingdom order for the marriage because the marriage at home will have an impact on those who will minister and operate under kingdom authority and anointing.

Genesis 2:7
And the Lord God formed man of the dust of the ground, and breathed into his nostrils the breath of life; and man became a living soul.

In Genesis 2:7, we note that God formed man. We need to pay close attention to the word *formed*. The word *formed* is the Hebrew word *yatsar* (yaw-tsar'), which means "to squeeze into shape." Another lexicon gives the meaning of "pressing as to put something into a tight place." God formed man or squeezed or pressed man into shape.

> *Genesis 2:21-23*
> *And the Lord God caused a deep sleep to fall upon Adam and he slept: and he took one of his ribs, and closed up the flesh instead thereof; [22] And the rib, which the Lord God had taken from man, made he a woman, and brought her unto the man. [23] And Adam said, This is now bone of my bones, and flesh of my flesh: she shall be called Woman, because she was taken out of Man.*

The Lord formed man; however, in Genesis 2:22 He *made* the woman. The word *made* is the Hebrew word *banah* (baw-naw') which means "to build or repair." This word also means "one who obtains children." Remember, the Lord formed the man, meaning he squeezed man into shape, but the Lord made or built the woman. Not only did God make or build her but made her to be able to obtain children. What are you seeing in the spirit? God built the woman that she might fit the man. Prophetically speaking, God builds the woman to fit the man's call and ministry. God must build the woman according to the call and anointing of the gift of the man. Kingdom marriages were positioned to be able to fit together as it pertains to the work of the kingdom. God formed the man, but He built the woman for the man. God called you both, but both have to be made to fit together with the other; if not, the enemy will use the unfitted part of the marriage to destroy the complete marriage.

Those of you considering marriage have many things to consider. This is where prayer comes in. I would place my proposed mate on the altar of the Lord, and if God does not resurrect that person, then leave that person there. It means that it is not the piece that will fit where God is taking you. When the gifted couple understands, then they will understand how relevant their call is as it pertains to the kingdom.

Prophetically speaking, the man of God carries the seed of vision while the woman carries the womb which is able to house that vision. Naturally speaking a man must go into a woman as Elkanah knew Hannah in order for that woman to become impregnated and to produce a child. We must get the spiritual application; spiritually speaking, a man of God who is called into kingdom ministry must go into his mate FIRST! What does that statement mean? The man of God must impregnate the one who was built according to the call upon his life; she becomes impregnated by her husband.

The woman was created by God to fit the ministry of the man. The woman is fashioned after the gift (apostolic call) of the man. The woman understands what God is doing, and she also recognizes the call. As the man of God speaks, she is the first to receive because she is first in his life. The man of God pours into or impregnates the woman. The woman then produces children, meaning she produces the effects of what is being preached; the wife or woman becomes the very message that her husband is preaching.

The major reason why there are so many divorces in the church is because no one understands their position both in the kingdom and in the home. My wife is my greatest support and encourager because God built her to fit me, and as God expands me, Glenda expands with me. Whatever I preach, teach, or write, she is first partaker because she becomes impregnated with what God is saying and doing through me; she then has children (in the spirit), her message becomes what she has been taught, and what she has been taught is what was put into her by her husband. Remember, the man must go into the woman. There is a part of my life and ministry that must enter into the life of my wife. God formed the man, but He built (banah) the woman, He made the woman to produce a child!

> *Gen. 2:20*
> *And Adam gave names to all cattle, and to the fowl of the air, and to every beast of the field; but for Adam there was not found an help meet for him.*

The woman is to become the helpmeet. What does this mean? The word for *meet* is the Hebrew word `ezer, which means a female helper; it also means one that is acceptable and meets the standard. A helpmeet is acceptable help in the area of the ministry.

Deal with Haman

> *Amos 3:3*
> *Can two walk together, except they be agreed?*

What about past issues? One of the greatest threats and arguments in marriages as a whole is the situation of past issues. In Amos 3:3, we note a question that is rhetorical, meaning it asks a question but within that question lies the answer. Can two walk together, except they be agreed? What is meant by the word *agreed*? The word *agreed* is the Hebrew word *ya`ad* (yaw-ad'), and it implies "to meet." Another meaning denotes two people coming to a tent of meeting and entering in. So this word literally means a meeting and entering into together. Can two walk together except they enter in together? Can two walk together in marriage except they enter into that marriage together, both physically and spiritually? Can two walk together in the Kingdom except they enter into that message together? The anointing of agreement is what produces the harvest in all that is done between the two individuals; however, the anointing of agreement is the most difficult for marriages to accept because the anointing of agreement will require for one person to agree and possibly give in.

Many feel as though dealing with past issues is not relevant, but in essence it is extremely relevant. The enemy's strength is the weakness of the believer. The enemy's strength to a marriage is any opening that will create controversy; whichever area is weak becomes potential for the enemy. The area of the marriage that has been skipped over per se must be dealt with regardless if it is a secular marriage or Christian marriages.

Any loophole or weakness in the marriage is potential for the enemy. Any area that has not been dealt with in the relationship is potential for an attack. When I played football with my childhood, friends we would always look for the weak side of the other team's offense, and once we would find it, that's the area that we would attack. Your past life prior to marriage can become a weakness and potential for the enemy; therefore, it is important to deal with those areas. This principle applies to those who function in the kingdom. As the kingdom begins to expand and your gift begins to be utilized, part of getting to that place of operation is making sure all is well.

Deal with your past issues so that they will not come back to haunt you. A mate should be one who you can share anything with and feel confident in that confidentiality and trust. To back up what I am saying, let us look at King Saul in the scriptures.

King Saul was commanded by the Lord through Samuel the prophet to utterly destroy all the Amalekites. Saul did not destroy all, and along with that he allows the king to live. Saul and the people kept some of the spoils of their enemy. When Samuel the prophet arrived, Saul began to say how the Lord had given the victory, but Samuel heard the sheep and inquired, "If you killed everything, what is that I hear?" Saul was disobedient and he did not utterly destroy all of the Amalekites; in essence, he did not deal with the situation properly. Saul eventually died, and a few hundred years later we learn of Esther. Esther was interceding on behalf of the Israelites because they were facing total annihilation by a man called Haman. Who was Haman? Haman was an Agagite (Est. 3:1), a descendant of Agag, who was the king of the Amalekites during Saul's reign (1 Sam. 15:8). Had Saul been obedient and dealt with the enemy when God told him to, the threat of annihilation at the hand of Haman would not have been possible. Had Saul the King dealt with Agag the king of the Amalekites, then Esther would not have had to deal with Haman. What am I saying? I'm saying that in regards to Kingdom ministry, those who are going to function on this level must deal with issues before the enemy notices the weak side and see the potential for creating havoc which will in turn create hindrance. If you deal with your Haman now, you will strengthen the weak side of your marriage. Down the road when you have become settled, the very thing that you refused to deal with may come back to haunt you. If you're going into ministry or feel the call of God upon your life, then you need to deal with your mate about it because the worse to happen is to get into ministry without the blessing and anointing of your mate. It will become a burden on top of burdens. Deal with the past issues, deal with the issue of your mate, and fully understand what God is doing.

God formed (*yatsar*) the man, and then he made (*banah*) the woman. Why? Because there must be the spirit of agreement in what we do, so she has to be made after what God has formed me into. God charged me as an apostle and He charged Glenda as well. When I stood before those men of God for affirmation, my wife was standing with me in the spirit. As I was being elevated, my wife was being elevated. We had to enter into this call "AGREED." Yes, God had to give me someone who He made for me and my call; Glenda is made according to not only me but my call. If Glenda does not understand the call upon my life, she could become the greatest hindrance in my life, and it will affect me so that I will only go but so far in the kingdom.

My wife may not understand everything concerning my call, and I'm sure she has questions; however, she must always honor that call; she must submit herself to what God is doing through me. I must also submit to her and her call to the kingdom as well. I must become her greatest support; I must become the message of her ministry. In essence, we both push and support each other in the ministry

To my brothers and sisters who are reading this writing, I pray that this writing has provoked you to seek the face of God as never before. Maybe there are some who are in a marriage and are headed down the path of divorce. I pray that this writing would serve as a help in order to get you both to focus on what God is calling forth.

Your service to the kingdom is needed and to those who understand this, if you obey, then your gift will cause you to excel very far because you considered the kingdom first, and when you consider the kingdom first then all these other things will be added. In other words, you considered the kingdom to the degree that you called on the Father to build your ministry and the relationship of your mate that is connected to the ministry and everything that is connected to you.

Can two walk together except they be agreed? In regards to the Kingdom, can a marriage function in the kingdom under the one umbrella of agreement? Can the Agreed be the chosen unit that God had called for? Can such a unit be released making havoc in the kingdom of darkness? I say yes, yes they can. The two prophetically must become one and in the spirit of oneness flow in the spirit of anointing not only in the kingdom but in the marriage at home and all that their kingdom and marital relationship are connected to.

The Prophet's Posture
"Put off Thy Shoes"

As the kingdom expands and moves in the power of the Holy Ghost, the Father is about to release a fresh order of prophets. The releasing of the prophets will require a season and time of preparation; it will require that the prophet prior to being released stay in a certain posture. This chapter is entitled the Prophet's Posture, and in this chapter we will prophetically reveal the position the prophets must take prior to being released within the kingdom and the world.

Inspired communication from God comes through His prophets. Who are His prophets? His prophets are men and women of God who speak under the unction and inspiration of the Holy Spirit. In Luke 11:49, Jesus said that He would send the prophets and apostles. Prophets are those who operate under an apostolic anointing. They are sent to the kingdom and are set within the kingdom by God (Eph. 4:11). Prophets are in relationship and communion with the Lord. They know the Word of God, the plan and purposes of God, and they speak what is in the heart and mind of God.

Prophecy is the vehicle which God uses to get His word from His throne into the earth realm, and it is in this sense that the prophet is utilized. The Father speaks a Word outside of time in Eternity, and that word must get to the earth; the prophet is the vessel that God uses to bring His word out of eternity by speaking into His prophet, who in turn speaks that word into time and into an individual.

> *Isaiah 55: 11*
> *So shall my word be that goeth forth out of my mouth: it shall not return unto me void, but it shall accomplish that which I please, and it shall prosper [in the thing] whereto I sent it.*

When a prophet delivers a word into the earth, which in most cases is to an individual, once that individual receives that word that word begins to make its way back to God. The individual who received that word must align himself or herself with that word (catch it) because it is consistently moving back to the Father. The Bible reads in Isaiah 55:11 that the word that goes from His mouth in eternity shall not return unto Him void. That word *void* means "empty or useless." Every word that comes out of the mouth of God has a purpose, and that purpose is to cause His people to prosper. Once the prophet delivers that Word, that word begins to work its way back to the Lord, and when that word returns unto the Lord, it would have served its purpose. The Word becomes the individual and that individual becomes that spoken word. Both the word and the individual then at one point in the believer's life will return to the Lord, and it is at that time that the believer will not return unto Him void, empty, or without purpose. You would have served out your purpose by obeying the prophetic word. This is initiated by the prophet of God

The job of the prophet is to declare, tell forth, or reveal the word of the Lord. The anointing of the Holy Spirit is released upon a prophet in order that he may prophesy. Where does this unction take place? Jesus said in John 7:38, *"He that believeth on me, as the scripture hath said, out of his belly shall flow rivers of living water."* Out of his belly: the word *belly* is the Greek word *koilia* (koy-lee'-ah), meaning his "abdomen," but figuratively speaking, the belly is the heart or one's innermost being. The unction to prophesy is felt in ones innermost being. There are some today who feel as though they are prophets; however, they have no call, no charge, no training, no unction, and most importantly they have no word flowing out of their innermost being.

> *1 Samuel 19:20*
> *And Saul sent messengers to take David: and when they saw the company of the prophets prophesying, and Samuel standing as appointed over them, the Spirit of God was upon the messengers of Saul, and they also prophesied.*

The office of the prophet is one that has been abused. In these times when an individual has guessed something concerning an individual who may need ministering because the individual guessed right, that person is declared a prophet by those who don't understand the prophetic, yet the individual has not been called to be a prophet. We miss a very important fact concerning prophets, and in I Samuel 19:20 we learn of an important order. In 1 Samuel 19:20 there was a company of prophets prophesying, and Samuel was standing as appointed over them. Notice Samuel was appointed over them (the prophets). This teaches that the prophets were accountable to someone. A prophet will be subject to someone who in turn will give them validation. It must be understood that today's prophets must go through a process of being trained.

Many so-called prophets today have made a mess of things in the name of God. Their mess has caused many believers to be leery of the prophetic gift. Today the Father is about to release prophets in the Kingdom, and those prophets will be sensitive to the Spirit of the Lord. They will be sensitive to erroneous and false teaching, and they will recognize and judge spirits of divination and false prophecy.

There are no more Lone Rangers; the prophetic company will be released. What is meant by the term "the prophetic company?" The prophetic company consists of the Apostle, Prophet, Evangelist, Pastor, and teacher. The prophetic company is the Five-fold Ministry, the Hand of the Lord.

Ezek. 37:1
The hand of the Lord was upon me, and carried me out in the spirit of the Lord, and set me down in the midst of the valley which was full of bones

In my book entitled "Can These Bones Live," I talk about the Apostolic Company. Prophetically speaking, in Ezekiel 37:1, the hand of the Lord represents the Five Fold Ministry, also known as the apostolic company. The apostolic company is not an organization but a particular order in God, which reveals that all five gifts are in company with each other. No gift is better than the other because all are needed to make up the Hand of the Lord.

Ezekiel speaks of the Hand of the Lord being not under him but upon him. The hand being upon him reveals that Ezekiel was under the hand of the Lord. Each gift of the hand of the Lord must be willing to function under one another. The Hand then carried Ezekiel out, which denotes the gift of the prophet. It was the gift needed to be in operation at that time; however, the whole hand was there (in company) with the prophetic gift. The kingdom will require more than just one gift; it will take more than one finger to cause the Kingdom of God to do what God is calling forth today. The gift that was needed at this time in Ezekiel 37 is the prophet; please keep in mind that though all gifts were represented there, the one that needed to be in operation at that time was the prophet.

Once again within the Kingdom, the Lord is stretching forth His hand and releasing what is needed in the Kingdom for the sake of the Kingdom and the world. The prophet is needed and the prophets being released today will have to sit among seasoned prophets in order to receive wise council concerning the kingdom of God.

The calling forth of prophets will require a certain posture. That posture is noted in Exodus 3:5 which reads *"And he said, Draw not nigh hither: put off thy shoes from off thy feet, for the place whereon thou standest [is] holy ground."* God told Moses, "not" to draw nigh. In other words, do not come closer. Why couldn't Moses draw closer? The reason is because there was a requirement from God prior to Moses' stepping up into a higher realm. Moses was stepping up into an experience that he has never seen before, and he was not to rely on anyone or anything to give him understanding as to what God was getting ready to reveal. The scripture goes on to say, *"Put off thy shoes from off thy feet."* Moses was told to take off his shoes. Why the removal of the shoes? The shoes were responsible for getting Moses from Egypt to the desert, they were responsible for getting him to this place in his life, and, prophetically speaking, those shoes had taken him as far as they could. The shoes were able to give Moses natural direction; however, he needed something different because God was calling Moses into something different. It was something higher and greater for the sake of the Kingdom. Moses had to remove his shoes; the element that has carried him for the last 80 years was to be taken off!

To the prophet of this day may I speak prophetically that the course you are about to take concerning the kingdom is one that you have never taken before. No seminary can prepare you for what the Father is about to do through you; however it will take an aligning with a seasoned apostolic gift within the Kingdom. Your shoes, though they are nice ones, absolutely must come off because prophetically you are about to go to another dimension in Him. The higher dimension is necessary, and the preparation for that dimension will be that much more demanding. Your shoes have brought you to this point in your prophetic walk. Now its time to take them off.

> *Jonah 1:3*
> *But Jonah rose up to flee unto Tarshish from the presence of the LORD, and went down to Joppa; and he found a ship going to Tarshish: so he paid the fare thereof, and went down into it, to go with them unto Tarshish from the presence of the LORD.*

Jonah was a prophet who disobeyed the Lord. The Lord told Jonah to go to Nineveh; however, Jonah went to Joppa instead. Why did

Jonah disobey the Lord? Let us learn a little history concerning Nineveh. Nineveh was the meanest Gentile city in the world at that time. The Assyrians ruled Nineveh, and it was the Assyrians who invented the punishment called impalement. What was impalement? It is when the Assyrians would take a stake about 9 feet long and put it in the ground and take the troublemakers and enemies and stick them on top of the stakes. After about 1 or 2 days the individual would eventually slide down the stake with the stake protruding through them. Those stakes were all around the city of Nineveh, and the bodies were on them. This type of punishment served as a warning from the Assyrians to say that if you messed with us, this would happen to you. Nineveh was a cruel city, and this is what Jonah had to see when he went to Nineveh, and it probably produced some concerns with Jonah. Many will have to go to Nineveh and face barbaric situations; however, during your time and season of preparation, the Father will prepare and anoint you for what you will face. Jonah disobeyed the voice of the Lord, caught a boat, and took it to Joppa, which was in Tarshish. While on his way, a terrible storm arouse, and Jonah ended up being thrown overboard and was swallowed by a large fish.

    Jonah remained in the belly of the great fish for three days. It was during that time that he had to repent. He being in the belly of the fish for three days denotes a time when he was able to reflect, to deal with the chastening of God and prepare for his call. The call and charge are the same, however, Jonah must get in spiritual and apostolic shape in order to deliver a word, and that preparation for the prophet is seen in him being in the belly of the fish.

    Moses was to take off his shoes, Jonah was in the belly of a fish for three days, but when both these prophets emerged, what God did through them was earth shattering. Moses led millions out of Egypt, Jonah preached a word that caused a complete city to repent, fast and pray including the King of that city. The posture of the prophet is spending time in the presence of the Lord with shoes off and in the belly totally shut off from the world and its surroundings. The prophet today must be totally submitted to the cause of the Kingdom. The process will require that God totally make you ready, and when you are ready, the people will know for not a word that God speaks into you will fall to the ground.

    The Respect and honor of the Office are returning

1 Samuel 2:12
Now the sons of Eli were sons of Belial; they knew not the Lord.

The sons of Eli were called "sons of belial." The word *belial* means "without profit, worthlessness, destruction or wickedness." The sons of Belial are those in ministry who are wicked, worthless, and full of destruction. The sons of Belial seek to function in ministry. It is a spirit of anti-Excellence which attempts to over rule the order of the Lord and to disrupt that order. The spirit of Belial will function amongst men and women in ministry who show no respect or regard to the priesthood or the prophetic office. Belial is a spirit which is alive today, and that spirit has caused the gift of the prophet to be disrespected. This is a spirit that is running rampant throughout the earth. It has caused many to not believe in God's prophets; however, God is restoring the confidence of the people concerning His prophets. Upon being processed, the prophet released in the kingdom for this day will understand the importance of the prophetic office along with its honor and respect.

1 Samuel 16:4
And Samuel did that which the Lord spake, and came to Bethlehem. And the elders of the town trembled at his coming, and said, Comest thou peaceably?

In 1 Samuel 16:4 Samuel went down to Bethlehem to Jessie the father of David's house. Notice the action of the elders towards Samuel. The Bible reads that the elders trembled. The word trembled is the Hebrew word *charad* (khaw-rad'), which means "to shudder with terror; to fear." The elders saw Samuel and just the presence of Samuel brought fear to the city. This denotes that Samuel was a prophet not to be reckoned with.

1 Kings 18:,7-9
And as Obadiah was in the way, behold, Elijah met him: and he knew him, and fell on his face, and said, Art thou that my lord Elijah? [8] And he answered him, I am: go, tell thy lord, Behold, Elijah is here. [9] And he said, What have I sinned, that thou wouldest deliver thy servant into the hand of Ahab, to slay me?

In 1 Kings 18:4-9, when Obadiah met up with Elijah, Obadiah fell on his face and asked if the prophet was Elijah. When Elijah answered, Obadiah was sore afraid and began to inquire if the prophet was there to see him. Again there was such a reverence for the prophet of God.

1 Kings 18:17
And it came to pass, when Ahab saw Elijah, that Ahab said unto him, Art thou he that troubleth Israel?

When the prophet Elijah saw Ahab the king, Ahab asked Elijah "A*re thou he that troubleth Israel?*" Notice again that Ahab asked Elijah was he the one that troubleth Israel. The word *troubleth* is the Hebrew word `akar (aw-kar'), which means "to disturb, afflict, or stir." Elijah's gift was so powerful that he stirred up and afflicted Israel. The respect and honor of the prophetic gift is returning to the prophets as it will be noted in this fresh release of the men and women of God. The people of God will in this day of the Kingdom look upon the prophets with reverence as the mouthpieces of God.

Deut. 32:11
As an eagle stirreth up her nest, fluttereth over her young, spreadeth abroad her wings, taketh them, beareth them on her wings.

This paragraph was taken from my book entitled "Can These Bones Live?" For what the Lord is speaking on these pages I feel bears repeating. This is concerning the prophetical gift. "The habitat of the prophet is in the presence of God. Where is God? He is above. *'For thou, Lord, art high above all the earth: thou art exalted far above all gods'* (Psalms 97:9). Every prophet must live above the earth realm in the presence of the Lord. The prophet is represented by the eagle in Deuteronomy 32:11. Notice the eagle "stirreth" up her nest. The Hebrew word for *stirreth* is *uwr* which means, 'To open up the naked (spiritual) eyes.' The prophet causes the believers within the kingdoms eyes to come open and see the purpose of God. *'Doth the eagle mount up at thy command, and make her nest on high? She dwelleth and abideth on the rock, upon the crag of the rock, and the strong place. From thence she seeketh the prey, and her eyes behold afar off. Her young ones also suck up blood: and where the slain are, there is she'* (Job 39:27-30). The eagle (prophet) dwells or lives upon a Rock. That Rock is Christ and makes her abode on high. Remember, the prophet must live up in God. His abode or habitat is up on high upon the Rock. Living up on the

Rock on high, the eagle (prophet) is able to see afar off and down where the downtrodden and dead are. The eagle (prophet) picks them up (by way of prophetic utterance; a Word from the Lord) and brings those that are broken and those that are dead to where the prophet resides. Where does the eagle live? The eagle (prophet) resides on the Rock up above in the presence of God." The prophet is about to be released; however, that releasing will not come without the prophet settling in a particular posture. In that posture, he will receive instruction. The seasoned prophets will teach, instruct, and coach the younger prophets. It will be necessary so that the younger prophets can understand the relevance of why they are called at this time within the kingdom.

The prophet will need to remove his shoes; the prophet will need to sit in the belly of a fish for some days; the prophet cannot live down among the low thinking of the people but must live up on the Rock, which denotes a place of separation and dedication.

The prophet will respect the call and walk in the respected and honored call. Because the prophet will honor the call and respect the call, the kingdom will respect and honor the prophet. Not a word that God speaks from eternity into the prophet will fall to the ground. There will be no hitting and missing of a prophetic word. The people will not have to wonder if is it off God or not, for the anointing upon the life of the prophet will make its words to be made known. Those words will be able to go down to the downtrodden and swoop them up and place them in their place of destiny.

The task of the prophet in this day will be to go by many waysides and many dunghills and retrieve those who have been thrown away and cast into the garbage. The garbage speaks of those who have been thrown out and discarded by an ungodly church system. The dunghill was a place where the depressed lived. It was a stinky place, a horrible place, and, most importantly, a place of humiliation and embarrassment. The task of the prophet will be to go to those places and swoop up those who are there and to bring them back to purpose.

This is why the posture of the prophet is extremely important. The posture of the prophet has to do with the processing of that prophet. These are the men and women of God who have been hidden by the many Obadiah's and watched over and trained by the Samuels of today. The prophet's posture is a position the prophet must take in order to be released into the kingdom in these last days. The prophet's posture is a position from which God will prepare His prophet to be able to function and carry an anointing consistent with what God wants to do on earth. The anointing will be a former and latter anointing in the same month. That speaks of a preparation-anointing and a harvest-anointing at the same time. The prophet has got to be prepared to walk in such an anointing, and this is the reason for the prophet's posture.

The Authority in Being Sent

Hebrews 11:3
Through faith we understand that the worlds were framed by the word of God, so that things which are seen were not made of things which do appear.

What came first? Was it faith or was it word? The worlds were framed not by faith but by the Word of God. The word for *word* is the Greek word *rhema* (hray'-mah), which means "an utterance, sound; series of words joined together into a sentence; a declaration of one's mind made into words." The word *rhema* means "a declaration of one's mind made into words." The worlds were framed by God speaking His mind. Out of what God spoke which was word, came faith. Faith was not needed in creation; faith is needed for men to believe that God created.

Rhema is what God said. It denotes something that was thought and has manifested. Rhema literally is the will of God spoken out, and it establishes divine order.

Divine order is God's divine, accurate, unchangeable arrangement in regards to His purpose, which cannot be altered. It is the most important word in the kingdom. Disorder invokes another spirit whereas divine order invokes the very presence of God. Rhema establishes divine order, which is the means by which the kingdom operates.

The divine order is the "sent" order. Anything that is sent denotes a purpose for it being sent, and it also denotes a destination and a function. The Kingdom-oriented people operate under the divine order. They operate under the order of "sent," which means they have a purpose and destination which can not be altered. In that order consists an anointing for that particular assignment. The word requires faith when it operates in the earthly realm; faith manifests the word, which manifests divine order, which manifests results. This all manifests itself only in the confines of "sent."

What is meant by the authority of being sent? When the Father sends something, that which is sent carries a particular authority. Wherever the Father sends a word, that particular word comes with authority, and when faith is revealed in the recipient of that particular sent thing, that sent thing does what it was sent to do.

> *Matthew 8:5-10*
> *And when Jesus was entered into Capernaum, there came unto him a centurion, beseeching him, [6] And saying, Lord, my servant lieth at home sick of the palsy, grievously tormented. [7] And Jesus saith unto him, I will come and heal him. [8] The centurion answered and said, Lord, I am not worthy that thou shouldest come under my roof: but speak the word only, and my servant shall be healed. [9] For I am a man under authority, having soldiers under me: and I say to this man, Go, and he goeth; and to another, Come, and he cometh; and to my servant, Do this, and he doeth it. [10] When Jesus heard it, he marvelled, and said to them that followed, Verily I say unto you, I have not found so great faith, no, not in Israel.*

In Matthew 8:5-10 there is to be learned a beautiful application concerning the authority of being sent. We see the story concerning a centurion. A centurion was an officer in charge of at least eighty men (soldiers). The centurion came to Jesus on behalf of his servant who was sick of palsy and was grievously tormented. Jesus said he would go and heal the servant but the centurion told Jesus that his roof was not worthy for Jesus to come under. Then the centurion said something profound; he said, "I am a man under authority" meaning the centurion understood the importance of submission or being under an authority. Submission accompanies purpose, and if one cannot submit, then one cannot function in Godly purpose. The centurion has submitted to the authority of the purpose for which he was sent. He did what he was sent to do, and because of that, he carried an authority along with he serving his purpose in the Roman Army.

Just as the centurion was sent to do a particular job, so was Jesus sent to do a particular job and because Jesus was sent, the authority that accompanies one being sent accompanied His purpose. The centurion was under an authority; he was sent to do a particular task and was expected to do what he was sent to do. The authority of being sent means that though one is sent, there is an authority that accompanies that sending.

Jesus marveled and said, "*I have not found not so great faith, no, not in Israel.*" Though the centurion was not of the house of Israel, he understood a Godly principle. The principle is that if God sends something, He authorizes that who is sent and equips that which is sent in order to complete the task. Another of the principles that Jesus saw in the centurion was the principle of obedience, to do what you are called upon to do and do it to the fullest.

The authority of being sent is authorized power that accompanies your calling or placement wherever the Father places you. God designates a place where He desires for His word to be manifested. The designated place in Matthew chapter eight was the centurion's servant; the designated place for you the believer may be a third world country, a desolate place that will need a fresh word from the Lord. The designated place is anywhere the Father wills, for His will to be done.

Psalms 107:20 reads, *"He sent his word, and healed them, and delivered them from their destructions."* The word *sent* is the Hebrew word *shalach* (shaw-lakh'), which in the Hebrew Lexicon means "a projectile." A projectile is "something that is maneuvered and released accompanied by a driving forward force attempting to reach a target. "He sent his word" means the word was aimed and then released with a driving force with the intention of hitting its target. When He sent his word in Psalms 107:20, it meant He aimed His word at a specific target and it hit. The results of that hit were that the word accomplished what it was sent to do: it healed and delivered them. Anything sent from God is a projectile and it has the intention of hitting its target. As previously discussed, the centurion was an man under authority; it means that he was sent, he was aimed, and what accompanied that sent thing was the force or the authority of those who sent him.

The Word is a driving force sent from God functioning under the authority of He who sent that Word. The environment into which the word is being sent must be conducive to the Word, meaning the environment for the sent word must be that of faith because the sent thing from God can not operate in anything that has not been sanctioned by God.

Faith operates in the earth. Faith clears the ground, it moves all mountains and obstacles of doubt; it moves any hindrances; faith gets the individual ready for a sent word and the manifestation of that word. Many churches and believers are misinformed. Jesus told us to seek the kingdom not seek all of the stuff. Stuff will crowd the path for the sent Word and manifestation of that word. Paul said he is not ashamed of the Gospel of Christ for it is the power of God unto salvation, meaning, that when the sent word comes to a situation where God has sanctioned, the word will be in full demonstration because the word was sent and the authority of that word accompanied the word. The designated place is full of faith waiting for that word to hit the mark!

The kingdom mode of operation is a sent mode. The kingdom was sent and has come. It was sent or shot into the earth by the Father, and the kingdom is to function with the authority that accompanies it. Faith is in the atmosphere, which allows the Word to function without hindrance.

> *Acts 16:16*
> *And it came to pass, as we went to prayer, a certain damsel possessed with a spirit of divination met us, which brought her masters much gain by soothsaying:*

In Acts 16:16-18 there was a damsel who was possessed with a spirit of divination. With that spirit she was able to make her masters a lot of money by means of soothsaying. Soothsaying was fortunetelling that is controlled by the spirit of divination. The spirit of divination is a principality that operates and functions in the earth realm. The word divination is the Greek word *Puthon* (poo'-thone), which is derived from the word *Putho*. Putho was the name of the region where a famous oracle named Delphi was located. An oracle is a person utilized by a demonic force through which those forces are able to speak. Divination is that spirit that operates through an individual being utilized by demonic forces in order to give information. The damsel operated under this ungodly anointing. However, the apostle Paul was on assignment, he was functioning under the "sent' authority.

> *Acts 16:18*
> *And this did she many days. But Paul, being grieved, turned and said to the spirit, I command thee in the name of Jesus Christ to come out of her. And he came out the same hour.*

When Paul noticed the damsel he said to that spirit in her "*I command thee in the name of Jesus Christ to come out of her.*" The Bible reads "*And he came out the same hour.*" That spirit came out because regardless of how powerful it was there was an authority operating that was greater than the spirit of divination. The word was operating in the environment that it was sent to; the word was aimed at that young damsel and it accomplished its mission by hitting the target. Paul was the vehicle that was in the position for the word to operate through. He was in a position so that the word could flow through without any hindrances.

1 John 3:8
He that committeth sin is of the devil; for the devil sinneth from the beginning. For this purpose the Son of God was manifested, that he might destroy the works of the devil.

The kingdom functions under the authority of being sent. The kingdom was aimed and shot out from heaven to earth. It is aimed at a particular area, which is the works of the devil. The kingdom is here to destroy the works of the devil. This will be accomplished this day through the kingdom. The authority will accomplish the mission, and it will be "mission accomplished."

Your Kingdom Gift

One of the most important things to know concerning an individual is who he is. If a person is known and understood, then the value of that individual is known and understood. In relationships whether Christian or secular, it is important to understand and know the value of the individual you are in a relationship with. Many can love and yet not understand the value of that person, and if the value is not understood and honored, then the gift of that individual will not be honored.

Your gift is what God gives you to impact the kingdom and the world; the Father also gives you the ability to operate in that gift. Purpose is one's reason for existing, and kingdom purpose is one's reason for existing in the kingdom. Your gift is a means for you to make an impact on earth, and in order to make a true impact, the first thing needed to be understood is knowing your gifting and calling and then honoring them by functioning in them to the fullest. The kingdom will know your calling by how you live, for your purpose will become your life.

> *2 Samuel 7:8-9*
> *Now therefore so shalt thou say unto my servant David, Thus saith the Lord of hosts, I took thee from the sheepcote, from following the sheep, to be ruler over my people, over Israel: [9] And I was with thee whithersoever thou wentest, and have cut off all thine enemies out of thy sight, and have made thee a great name, like unto the name of the great men that are in the earth.*

Understanding one's value calls for an understanding of what God is doing. In 2 Samuel 7:8-9, the Lord spoke through His prophet that He had made David's name great. The misconception of many is that they attempt to make their own name great and they attempt to create a great name through their gift. Many feel that because they have a gift, that the gift will make their name great, and if the name becomes great then the success will come. This is a great misconception, for only God makes your name great and if a name is made great by God, it is a name that will be eternal.

> *2 Cor. 4:7-10*
> *But we have this treasure in earthen vessels, that the excellency of the power may be of God, and not of us. [8] We are troubled on every side, yet not distressed; we are perplexed, but not in despair; [9] Persecuted, but not forsaken; cast down, but not destroyed; [10] Always bearing about in the body the dying of the Lord Jesus, that the life also of Jesus might be made manifest in our body.*

There are many who have passed away; their accomplishments during their life time were enormous, yet they never sought for a great name: Men such as Watchman Nee, who became a prisoner simply because of his confession of faith; Bishop Charles Mason, founder of the Church of God in Christ; and William J. Seymour, who played an important part in the Azusa meeting only to name a few. These men have all passed on; however, their names are great even until this day because God made their names great. Though they have passed on, their works have touched millions of lives and still continue to do so. God made their names great because they understood their purpose and value to the kingdom.

I have not read of men such as Watchman Nee, Smith Wigglesworth or Bishop Charles Mason attempting to market themselves in order to be famous. They did not utilize their God-given gifts in order to "get paid." They utilized their God-given ability to impact the kingdom and the world; they were "sold out." They endured much affliction in order to bring the Gospel to the lost.

Your gift is what God has given you to make an impact both in society and the world. Your kingdom gift will fit perfectly in the kingdom but will need to be validated to function. Your gift in the kingdom will call for your focus, attention, heart, and passion because it will affect men and women. Always remember that anything kingdom-oriented will affect men and women, and your kingdom-oriented gift will touch, change, motivate and challenge lives.

> *Proverbs 18:16*
> *A man's gift maketh room for him, and bringeth him before great men.*

The gift that God has graced you with is what you offer back to God. Yes, when you offer your gift unto the Lord, this is done by functioning to the fullest, bringing glory to God; as you bring your gift unto the Lord the Lord in turn expands your territory. He sees that you have valued and honored what He has graced you with. The Father then expands your territory which in turn brings you into the presence of great men. This does not mean you have "made it." It simply means that because you have valued your ability, God honored you for valuing or honoring that gift and has placed you before great men in order to represent God Himself. When you appear before great men, your purpose for that appearing will be utilized to the fullest. The greatness of that platform will not diminish your call; it will cause your gift to shine the more for the glory of God the Father.

In regards to the kingdom as a whole, believers must learn the importance of honoring and valuing each other. If we understand each other's value within the kingdom, then we will also understand each other's worth to the kingdom and in doing so will cause the Father to be glorified.

Isaiah 55:11
So shall my word be that goeth forth out of my mouth: it shall not return unto me void, but it shall accomplish that which I please, and it shall prosper in the thing whereto I sent it.

It is important to remember that we are placed here for a reason. God has gifted us and also has given us the ability to accompany that gifting. One of the most important chapters in this book is the chapter concerning time. Previously I stated that time must be filled with your purpose or your reason for existing. The Father asked me a question one night as I was preparing for Bible study. He asked, "If you had to stand before Me now, what could you tell Me your accomplishments were?" The question startled me and I brought the same question to Bible Study. The aforementioned men's works preach for themselves; their accomplishments actually are too far and great to number; however, they did make an impact. What they accomplished changed millions of lives. What impact have we made? What will people say concerning your accomplishments and impact when you are gone? What will be the one thing that will remind people of the impact you have made in the kingdom? If you closed your eyes and passed into eternity and had to stand before God, what could you tell God of your accomplishments on earth as it pertains to the kingdom? In all that you have done, if God called you home now, what could you tell Him if you stood before Him that pertains to the impact you have made in the earth? We who are of the kingdom must understand why we do what we do and the reason behind what we do.

Previously in the chapter entitled "Fulfilling the Time," I made the statement that God gives you the gift and what you need; however, there must be application of that ability which will bring success. God will deal with us according to the application of what we have been given. We need to examine just what we have accomplished and through those accomplishments ask ourselves, who that accomplishment has touched!

Time is filled with one's purpose, which is the kingdom-oriented charge from God to you, which will cause you to affect not only the kingdom but the world. The question now is what are we filling with time because what we fill with time is what must be given an account to God. What impact has your gift to the kingdom made?

> Matthew 7:22-23
> Many will say to me in that day, Lord, Lord, have we not prophesied in thy name? and in thy name have cast out devils? and in thy name done many wonderful works? [23] And then will I profess unto them, I never knew you: depart from me, ye that work iniquity.

What is your motivation? Why do you do what you do? Who gets the glory out of what you do? Many times we can become so involved with our ability never taking notice on just who has been touched, helped, blessed with that gift. Jesus said in Matthew 7:22-23, "Many shall come to Him in that day and say Lord, have we not prophesied in your name and cast out devils in your name and done many wonderful works in your name?" But then Jesus goes on to say that He would profess to them, "I never knew you: depart from me, ye that work iniquity." The word *knew* is the Greek word *ginosko* (ghin-oce'-ko), which means, "know" or "to have been made aware of." In other words, Jesus will say I've never been made aware of you. All that we do in the kingdom must bring praise, honor, and glory unto Him; if it does not, then He is not in it. He never knew what you are offering up because what you offer up does not reflect him. What is your motivation to do what you do? Your motivation must be Jesus.

Your kingdom gift must be handled as something of great value. Your kingdom gift is that which brings glory to the kingdom; however, we must remember that the gift must be a reflection of Jesus and in that we bring glory unto Him. The gift will not return unto the Lord void, meaning that the gift and all that God has given you to do in that day will speak for itself. If God was your motivation, then all that you accomplished in the name of the Lord will glorify Him and the gift will return unto the Father full of the Father's glory.

Men and women of God, we must find out why we have been born and function in that purpose. One of my favorite people in the Bible is a priest called Ahimelech. I mention him in many of my writings, and the reason is because we can be taught many things concerning this blessed man of God. Not much is known of him; there is not a chapter or book dedicated to him. However he teaches all of the people of God a very important lesson concerning value! He was a priest that was strategically placed by God. David was running from his spiritual father, Saul, and made it to the city of Nob. He arrived hungry and tired and with no defense, but upon his arrival someone was there to serve him. The person at Nob to serve David was a priest named Ahimelech. It was at this time that Ahimelech's purpose was known. He was created to be at a specific point in his life to feed David, and in doing so, not only did he restore David, but he fed the king and in essence prophetically, he ministered to David. Ahimelech teaches us the value of knowing who you are and functioning in it. His very position was vital for the future of the kingdom.

After David was restored, he left Nob, but King Saul arrived. Saul's men killed Ahimelech; he served his purpose and when his value was utilized and completed, he was killed by king Saul. The death of Ahimelech saved the life of the king. Ahimelech lived out his purpose, and he fulfilled his time. His life and accomplishment teach us that it is more important to be positioned to be utilized by God so that His plan will be revealed. So, Ahimelech will not return unto the Lord void but would have served his purpose. His gift of being a priest reflects all that God has prepared him for.

Honor each other's gift and understand the value of the gift, but, most importantly, know that your gift is to glorify God in whatever way He has determined or willed. I'll ask the question again. If the Father calls you home and asks you what have you done to make an impact in the kingdom, what will be your answer?

Keepers

Genesis 4:8-9
And Cain talked with Abel his brother: and it came to pass, when they were in the field, that Cain rose up against Abel his brother, and slew him. [9] And the Lord said unto Cain, Where is Abel thy brother? And he said, I know not: Am I my brother's keeper?

In one of my writings entitled "Words Defined Prophetically," there is a definition called Cain (spirit of), which is essentially a definition concerning the spirit of Cain and what that spirit represents. The spirit of Cain prophetically denotes the spirit of murder or character assassination. Cain was a son of Adam and Eve and brother to Abel. Cain became jealous of his brother Abel's offering unto the Lord and in his jealousy slew his brother Abel which then led to the Lord visiting Cain inquiring of his brother Abel.

In Genesis 4:9, God asked Cain a question that required an answer; actually, it was what we call a rhetorical question. A rhetorical question is a question that possesses its own answer. God asked Cain *"Where is Abel thy brother?"* Cain then answered, *"I know not, am I my brother's keeper?"* In the original it would read, *"Am I the guard of my brother?"* Note the difference: the KJV reads, "Am I my brother's keeper" However, in the original it reads, "Am I the guard of my brother?" Cain asked, Is it my job to guard my brother? It is not my intention to discuss the act of murder but we need to look at the position that Cain was to be in which was to be his brother's keeper. The question was rhetorical which denotes its own answer and the answer to Cain's question was absolutely yes.

In this chapter we are going to discuss something that is vital to not only the local church but to the kingdom. We are going to discuss a Keeper. Exodus 20:6 reads, *"And shewing mercy unto thousands of them that love me, and keep my commandments."* The word *keep* is the Hebrew word *shamar* (shaw-mar'), which denotes "a sheepfold of thorns." When a shepherd was out in the wilderness with his flock for the night, he would gather thorn bushes to build a hedge or cage to place his flock in order to protect that flock from predators. The protecting hedge of thorns denotes the idea behind the Hebrew word *shamar* which is translated *"guard."* In Exodus 20:6 the word *keep* is translated *guard* and should read, "and showing mercy unto thousands of them that love me and protect or *guard* my commandments." This particular passage speaks of an individual keeping, guarding or protecting the commandments of the Lord in their heart.

Numbers 6:24 reads, "The Lord bless thee, and keep thee." Again the word *keep* speaks of thorns serving as a hedge of protection. When the word "keep" is mentioned it speaks of protection so the passage should read, "The Lord bless thee and protect or guard thee." The word *keep* denotes protection so a keeper is one who protects. In the kingdom a keeper denotes the covering and protection of an individual prophetically, it carries the responsibility of spiritually watching over someone.

Romans 3:25
Whom God hath set forth to be a propitiation through faith in his blood, to declare his righteousness for the remission of sins that are past, through the forbearance of God;

In Romans 3:35, there is a word that deserves to be looked at in the scripture and that word is *forbearance*. The word *forebearance* is the Greek word *anoche* (an-okh-ay'), which means "self-restraint or tolerance." From the standpoint of being a keeper, the word *forebearance* means to be able to tolerate the part of an individual that has not matured, and, to pray for that area of immaturity in the individual's life. An example of this is if you are my brother I cover you in prayer, and at times you can be unknowingly offensive so I pray for the part of you that is offensive because that is the area of your life that has not matured. Forbearance requires that keepers do not throw a person aside because of their shortcomings, but, to watch over them, pray for them and in some situations give them wise counsel. A keeper is an intercessor who regardless of what an individual attempts to do or say, continues to pray and love that individual covering their immaturity and shortcomings in prayer.

Keepers not only forbear but are sold out. Keepers are those who are willing to give unto God whatever He desires as such is seen in the story known in the Hebraic as the Akedah. The Akedah story is the story of the binding up of Isaac by Abraham. The bible reads that Abraham saw the place afar off. The Hebrew word for place is *maqowm* which speaks of the exalted place, the third dimension, the place where full maturity is exhibited through the believer. The Akedah teaches us how God had given Abraham a gift in Isaac however, the gift was not so great that Abraham could not give it back. The Akedah teaches prophetically how those who are keepers within the kingdom do not hold anything back. The heart of Abraham is revealed through Abraham's obedience, yes that's not a typo, the Father already knew the heart of Abraham, but Abraham needed to know and, in that story, it teaches what the heart of a keeper is all about, its about giving regardless.

Pastors are keepers who go above and beyond. A keeper is a shepherd who keeps or protects the flock and they also posses the heart of God. A shepherd notes the sheep's shortcomings yet they take from themselves and give to the sheep. A shepherd has to endure the pain of the sheep yet a shepherd continuously keeps or protects the sheep because of the heart of that shepherd.

A shepherd does not retaliate because the heart of a shepherd does not retaliate; the heart of a shepherd loves those and prays for those who despitefully use the shepherd. Why is this? It is because of forebearance. The shepherd understands the sheep's shortcomings. In the kingdom keepers understand and forbear the one who has not matured.

Prophetic people are keepers. As previously stated, a keeper is an intercessor and intercessors are prophetic. Prophetic people are under the greatest attack from the enemy because they can see the enemy afar off and warn of the enemy. There are many so-called men and women of God who have no integrity but appear to be doing well; however, the keeper who is an intercessor appears to "go through" the worse because prophetic people stand at the front line of intercession and warfare.

Many desire to be prophetic, and many call themselves prophetic, however, they do not understand the sacrifice the prophetic calls for. A prophetic person is one who lives in a realm of God and becomes the revelation of God. A prophetic person sees God in the now and is full of faith. Prophetic people believe what they preach and teach. They become the epitome of that particular message. Many should understand what being prophetic entails and what that ministry requires. A prophetic person is a keeper, an intercessor, a shepherd, a lover of the people of God, and, most importantly, possesses the spirit of forebearance. So, if one desires to be a keeper or an intercessor he or she first must consider the sacrifice.

Being a keeper calls for much. You cannot only concern yourself with being prophetic because in the realm of being prophetic or a keeper, the rules are different then those who function in a realm of immaturity. The battle is greater and there will always be recourse from the enemy. A keeper is an intercessor that is prophetic but also walks a different lifestyle which is one of prayer and fasting, and because of the call, those who are keepers are connected to Five-Fold ministry; they are part of the apostolic company, walking in true apostolic anointing.

The extended hand of the Lord makes up the apostolic company which is not only the apostle, prophet, evangelist, pastor, or teacher, but also consists of helps, governments and offices that cause the kingdom and body of Christ to function as a whole. The extension of the five-fold ministry requires a connection to the five-fold ministry, which is prophetic. Everything that is connected to the five-fold must be prophetic, regardless of which area one serves.

If you have an apostolic leader, they who are connected to that leader must be of the same anointing; if the leader is prophetic then those who are connected to that leader must be prophetic. All that is connected with a prophetic leader becomes prophetic, and, therefore, the attack from the enemy towards that leader will also go towards those who are connected to the prophetic anointing. When the leader is under attack, those who are covered by that keeper will suffer the same however keepers (protectors) can war on behalf of their apostolic covering and connection.

Apostolic company means that the company is each other's keepers; the extended hand of the Lord which covers each other. Am I my brother's keeper? Am I the guard of my brother? Absolutely, yes. A keeper means one becomes another's hedge of thorns. A hedge of thorns is the spirit of prayer that covers lives; it is the *shamar* the thorn whereby when the enemy bucks up against a person covered he is pricked by the thorn of the spirit of prayer.

Getting to that place of a keeper, or *maqowm*, is not easy because it calls for process. The Father never meets you in the same place, meaning that when you were first born again, you were first dimensional, and the Father treated you as a babe. But eventually He will *kaleo* you, or call you by your name. He will call you *"anabaino hode"* which means, "to come up hither or "to leave that place in order to come up to this one." The Father calls you, the believer, to come up higher or move into a higher realm of the Spirit. Moving into a higher realm of the Spirit will call for more processing; however, the rules change. In the first dimension, you were easily provoked and became retaliatory, but what God called out of you in the first is greater in the second dimension. In the first dimension, you were retaliatory however, in the second dimension you have loved them that have retaliated against you. When the father moved you into the second dimension, He has brought you into a higher realm of maturity. It is in the second realm that He has sanctified you. The word *sanctified* is connected with the word Holy which means "to be cut out and separated from someone to someone." To be sanctified means that God has made you holy by cutting you away from a level of immaturity and bringing you into a higher realm of maturity. He cut you away from something, bringing you closer to someone, which is Him. Now the Father once again is calling you into a higher realm of maturity, which is the third dimension.

The third dimension is a hundred-fold manifestation which calls for another change of rules. The Father no longer deals with you as He did when you were immature and in the first dimension. The process has caused God to prepare you for your third dimension. The third dimension along with the change of rules causes you to love those who are immature in spite of; this is the realm of the keeper, the realm of the intercessor, the realm of those who understands forebearance. The third dimension causes one to look at an individual through the eyes of God; in this realm one is prophetic and is able to be a keeper and forebear. It is in this dimension of your walk with God that your life becomes a testimony being watched, admired, and fashioned by many who seek to come up hither.

> *Luke 22:42-45*
> *Saying, Father, if thou be willing, remove this cup from me: nevertheless not my will, but thine, be done. [43] And there appeared an angel unto him from heaven, strengthening him. [44] And being in an agony he prayed more earnestly: and his sweat was as it were great drops of blood falling down to the ground. [45] And when he rose up from prayer, and was come to his disciples, he found them sleeping for sorrow.*

Being a keeper is a profound and prophetic position within the kingdom. Those who are prophetic will suffer much this is why keepers can not go at it alone and need to be surrounded by other keepers. In other words intercessors should be surrounded and connected with other keepers or intercessors because of the recourse from the enemy through intercession. At this time within the kingdom, one should not war in the spirit alone but should do it with a company of believers.

A great relative and man of God whom I have admired and respected through the years is my cousin, Bishop Robert T. Robinson. Years ago, Bishop traveled to Africa, to preach and as he shared with me the stories and miracles that he witnessed through his ministering, he also told me something that I never forgot. He told me that the mistake out of that entire trip was that he traveled to Africa alone. Understand that Bishop went to the dark jungles of Africa where witch doctors rule and demonic forces manifested themselves in ways that we here in the US can only imagine. He said because of the forces that he faced, he should have never traveled to that place alone!

Intercession must be done corporately because of the recourse from the enemy. In Luke 22:42-45, Jesus was interceding in the garden, and He interceded to the point that His sweat was as drops of blood. Jesus was in agony because of the intercession and the impact of that prayer of intercession took its toll on Jesus. Because of this, Jesus needed ministering, and an angel from heaven came and strengthened, or ministered unto Him.

Notice in that passage of Scripture that Jesus brought three disciples with Him in order to watch (pray), but they fell asleep, and Jesus was left to intercede alone. This teaches that keepers must function in a corporate manor. Keepers must cover each other corporately because the prayer of protection will provoke a serious onslaught of attack from the enemy; however, corporately we will cover each other and ward off the attack. Note that when Jesus sent out the disciples He sent them out two by two. Never do warfare alone; keepers are corporate warriors who must remain awake in the Spirit so that they can cover the people of God and cover those who are not mature enough to cover themselves.

Keepers must walk alike, talk alike, think alike, if we are going to cover one another; then, spiritually, we must do things alike. If not, the attack of the enemy will come and attempt to cripple the believers as a whole. Keepers are those who stand in the gap; they close up the opening. The spirit of forebearance is the motivator of a keeper; the more they notice an individual's immaturity, the more a keeper covers.

Keepers are keepers of the flame. What is a keeper of the flame? The keepers of the flame are those who are intercessors who keep the fire on the altar lit. The altar is at the center of every ministry, and that flame must be kept (protected); it is the spirit of the intercessor that keeps the flame. Keepers of the flames are intercessors who keep the fire on the altar ablaze.

Keepers are corporate intercessors birthed in the kingdom. Keepers possess the heart of their shepherd (they have the same spirit as their pastor or leader). Keepers possess the heart of a shepherd, the spirit of forebearance, and the spirit of prayer. Keepers have a heart to give even when it hurts; they are Abrahams whose heart says that nothing is too great for the Father. The prayer life of a keeper is sharp and able to cover many. When they come under attack, the prayer will cover them, pricking the enemy. The position of a keeper is not the most popular or desired place within the kingdom; however, it is the most needed.

The Authority of the Kingdom

The Authority of the Kingdom is the rights, privileges, power and anointing given to the Church by the Father which allow His Church to function. In operating in that authority we understand our position and regardless of what may transpire we function as the Father has willed. Authority alone is not enough because kingdom citizens are balanced believers who not only function in authority but posses Godly character. Our character consists of the righteousness of God, the peace of God and the joy of the Holy Ghost. It is the anointing of God that equips the gifts within the kingdom enabling the believer to do a greater work. The anointing within the kingdom is a warfare anointing which allows the believer to war and pray for the many souls who have been lost by the wayside.

The Authority of the Kingdom exists in the glory of the Lord. The earth is full of His glory, meaning that the kingdom of God is full of the very person of God. The glory of the Lord denotes God being filled within His people and when released, releases an anointing to war, and also will produce a kingdom harvest. The harvest will come through the glory of the Lord, risen and revealed through His people.

The Authority of the kingdom will touch every dry, desolate area that suffered ruin. The River of God starts at the altar causing the water to gush out from under the altar. The spirit of prayer is the key to unlock this last day revival. The church must be ready to become the river. The River is a forward-moving authority that will touch the dry, deep, desolate places that are absent of the kingdom.

The River is created through the spirit of prayer which forms the people of God and also causes them to understand who they are. When individuals understands who they are then they also understand their reason for living, they understand their reason for existing, they understand their purpose. When ones purpose is understood then they can begin to fill the time. Remember, God will give you the ability, but He will not do the work for you. God will give you the gift, but then you must function in purpose. God gives the land; he'll give the seed; He will give you the ability but He will not give you application. Application happens when one begins to understand who he is.

The Authority is based upon one's obedience. The Bible tells us that disobedience is as the spirit of witchcraft. Authority calls for order; order calls for obedience. In our obedience we must never forget that Authority calls for a conforming. All that is out of order must be dealt with. All that is out of order in kingdom marriages must be dealt with. The marriage needs to be formed; the man of the marriage needs to be formed while the woman needs to be made. Let God do the forming and the making. If you allow God to form and make, it will develop the spirit of agreement.

The Authority of the Kingdom also requires that the inhabitants know their history. Legacy is extremely important because the kingdom of God is continuous; it does not cease to expand. Though many a believer will pass on, the expansion of the kingdom does not cease. Since the kingdom is constantly and will forever expand, it is important that the history of the kingdom be left on record. Knowing a legacy gives strength, encouragement, and power.

My pastor was a great woman of God who believed in the working of miracles, which I personally noted as a child. I remember the many nights I would sit at her kitchen table as she would rehearse some of the miracles that the Lord wrought through her ministry. My mother would also speak of the many miracles and ways that the Lord made when her back was against the wall. Many of those stories and testimonies have become part of my life. It is important to know where you come from. It is also important to know the direction the kingdom has come.

Kingdom Authority is to be passed down from one generation to another. As each generation takes up that authority, it becomes that much more powerful to that particular generation, therefore, generations must learn the importance of reverence and respect. Just as spiritual mothers and fathers of previous generations are respected, so must that authority be passed down, respected, and honored, and in our doing so will cause that authority to increase.

There is a special reverence; there is a recollection or a remembrance as it is important to never forget what God has done in previous generations. Once we understand this concept, then this generation will not have to do over the works of the kingdom that were previously carried out, but the Father will do a fresh thing in this generation.

What is a double portion? A double portion is a double portion of goods the first-born is to receive from his father. In Jewish history, the oldest male was to receive a double portion of the goods left to him by his father. Now, what is a double portion anointing? A double portion anointing operates on sons and daughters of spiritual fathers and mothers. When a son or a daughter takes over or continues a vision he or she receives the double portion anointing. The double portion anointing is the anointing of the spiritual father or mother in order to continue the work, and they receive the portion of anointing from the Father who anoints them to take the vision to another dimension, thereby receiving two or a double portion of anointing. The Authority of the Kingdom calls for the spiritual sons and daughters to take the kingdom to another level. A double portion anointing is the anointing that will equip this generation. So, history teaches where we have come from. It teaches how the Father has blessed and has made ways out of no way. Today, history becomes the encouragement that though faced with adversity we rely on what the Father has done in the past that will be done in an even greater way today.

Transition at times will bring change, and at times that change will seem like a digression. Digression can lead to disappointment, and disappointment to discouragement. Discouragement can then lead to setting the vision aside, and setting the vision aside can lead to burying that vision. Whenever transition becomes this devastating, you have to refer to your history to learn what was written aforetime for our learning.

Today it is important that the people of God get back into divine order, and in doing so they will cause the believers to understand just why they have been placed in the kingdom. They will recognize their gift, honor the gift, and, most importantly, display that gift for the kingdom.

God desires to be revealed today. He will be revealed when the people of God display the Authority of the Kingdom by operating in full authority. When the kingdom is operating in authority, we will see the "greater works." This will be done once the Body of Christ understands its rights, privileges, power, and anointing given to the Church by the Father. When we understand our position, regardless to what happens, we operate and function as the Father has willed His church to function. Authority alone is not enough. Kingdom citizens are balanced believers. Not only does the kingdom consist of authority, but character. Our character consists of the righteousness of God, and not only will the character of the kingdom be displayed, but the operation and authority of the kingdom will be displayed as a balanced kingdom of God.

"For thine is the kingdom, power and glory forever, Amen."

R.L. Robinson

About the Author

Dr. Robert Robinson is a speaker and teacher of church government and spiritual order as it pertains to a last day outpouring of God's anointing. In 1986, he entered the ministry and is presently the Senior Pastor of The House of Manna Ministries in Cranston, RI and is also the presiding prelate of the Rhema Covenant Fellowship. Dr. Robinson has authored over twenty-five books. Apostle Robinson is a Father and Pastor to many Pastors. He is married to his wife Glenda and both have been blessed with two children, David and Desere'. Dr. Robinson has traveled extensively throughout the United States in the ministry gift of an apostle, prophet, and teacher in churches, conventions, and seminars and continues to do so.

For information on other material by Dr. Robert Robinson Please contact
Dr. Robert L Robinson Ministries
PO Box 10106
Cranston, RI 02910
(401) 228-6108
Houseofmannaministries.com
Drrobinsonministries.com

Other Titles
By Dr. Robert Robinson

An Appointed Time
An encouragement to those who have been sidelined by the works of the enemy.

A Sevenfold Purpose
The Sevenfold Purpose is the revealing of the will of God to His church as it pertains to alignment and order.

A Survey of the Old Testament
This book gives information pertaining to the Old Testament. A survey of the Old Testament deals with the History of Israel, their Kings, prophets, priests and ordinances.

A Survey of the Old Testament Workbook
The workbook to A survey of the Old Testament

A Time to Work
This book serves as a word to believers concerning a period when God will release an anointing for seed and harvest.

Build Me A House
A motivational prophetic Word based on the book of Ezra.

Build Me A House Correspondence Course
Correspondence Course based on the book entitled "Build Me A House."

Can These Bones Live?
A writing based on the book of Ezekiel 37:1-14.

Hebrews Chapter Nine "The Interpretation"
This book is a verse by verse commentary on the ninth chapter of the book of Hebrews.

His Praise
This book teaches of the Hebrew Praise Words.

How we got the Bible
This book gives information concerning the history and makeup of the Bible. It deals with the many testing that were done in order to prove its authenticity.

How we got the Bible Workbook
This is the workbook to the book entitled "How we got the Bible." In it you will find questions that will assist you in developing an understanding for the history of the Bible.

Lessons I've Learned
This book is a compilation of bible studies taught by Dr. Robinson.

Revelation The Book
A commentary of the New Testament prophetical book of Revelations.

Revelation The Book Workbook
This is the workbook to "Revelation the Book."

The Authority of the Kingdom
This writing serves as a wakeup call to all believers in regards to what the Father has invested in the kingdom

The Ministry of the Tabernacle
This book is gives detailed information on the Tabernacle of Moses. This book includes the work book

The Ministry of the Tabernacle Workbook
The Workbook to the book The Ministry of the Tabernacle.

The Necessity for Leadership
This book deals with the need and importance of spiritual leadership.

The Numbers
The Numbers serves as a book of explanation of numbers throughout the Scripture.

Words Defined Prophetically
A dictionary to those who are new believers, students of scripture or seasoned believers. These words are those used in our everyday language within the Christian community and in ministry as a whole.

Made in the USA
Charleston, SC
12 December 2009

Made in the USA
Charleston, SC
12 December 2009